Creative SERGING FOR THE HOME
AND OTHER QUICK DECORATING IDEAS

Lynette Ranney Black
Linda Wisner

Edited by Barbara Weiland

Book design and production coordination by Linda Wisner

Room photography by Stephen Cridland
Close-up photography by Pati Palmer
Photo styling by Virginia Burney and Linda Wisner
Technical illustration by Kate Pryka and Melanie Pratt

We owe special thanks to all the associates and friends who contributed to this book. For donating not only their rooms, but also their talents, thanks to Marta Alto, Virginia Burney, Suzanne DeVall, Kelley Salber, and, especially, Barbara Weiland. And thanks also to Cleo Cummings and Susan Pletsch for letting us invade their homes! And to Pati Palmer for providing the opportunity to create this book, for putting up with the chaos of seamstresses coming and going, and for allowing us to use nine rooms in her historic home for these projects.

Thank you, too, to our interior seamstresses. We could not have done it without them!
Cheryl Elgin, Custom Interior Sewing; Kathryn Martin;
Marty Park, Park Place Creations;
Harriet Poore, Cloth Creations (slipcover specialist);
Ann Price; plus Rebecca Flaming-Martin, David Fones, Cindy Morgan, Rosemary Salber,
and quilter Olivia Harrison.

We also want to thank the people who graciously allowed us to use their prized possessions in our photography—to Kay Grasing for the silver used in the Victorian Tea; to Deborah Carnes for her antique Bauerware dishes used in the Sunny Breakfast Room and the Terrace; to artist Steven Fuller for his trompe l'oeil screen in the contemporary and ethnic living rooms; and most especially to Virginia Burney for the MANY perfect touches she added throughout the rooms in this book. Thank you also to Lynette's sister, Kelley Salber, for being there when we needed her.

Thank you also to the many companies who generously provided materials and assistance for the projects in this book. The Resource List on page 155 lists them all.

And more thanks to others who worked with us on this book—Harrison Typesetting, Inc.; photographer Stephen Cridland, whose ability to capture these rooms on film is unsurpassed; Steve's assistant's Kelly James; Kate Pryka, an illustrator with an exceptional ability to capture in drawings every sewing how-to we present to her; graphic artists/illustrators Melanie Pratt and Cheryl Reed; Linda Ellwanger, for her black & white photography; and to Wy'East Color and Craftsman Press.

The greyhound dog in our Veranda photo was provided by *Greyhounds for Pets*, an organization promoting retired greyhound racers as housepets. "One Spot" was a beautiful, gentle dog. For information, call (503) 232-3147.

We dedicate this book to our husbands, Paul Black and Bill Day, for their patience during this extensive project, and to Lynette's children, Kelsey and baby Jessica, who was born in the midst of the havoc!

Whenever brand names are mentioned, it is only to indicate to the consumer those products which we have personally tested and with which we have been pleased. It is also meant to save our students time. The brand names are listed in the Resource List, with appropriate trademark indications. There may be other products that are comparable to aid you in your home decorating sewing and serging.

Table of Contents

Foreword by Pati Palmer

There's a lot of excitement about home decorating AND about decorative serging today, so we decided to offer the home sewer the best of both in this beautiful book. It has taken nearly two years and the talents of the authors and numerous others to produce this exciting, one-of-a-kind book. I hope you'll enjoy scanning the pages again and again as you select ideas and projects for your home. I encourage you to use your serger, right along with your conventional machine, to make your home decorating projects fast and easy, not to mention beautifully decorative!

If it's difficult to find enough time to sew everything for your home, make the simpler items yourself and hire a professional to do the rest. I did this for my slipcovers and draperies. To make it easier than ever to find a pro, I am excited to announce the formation of PACC, the Professional Association of Custom Clothiers. Some of its members specialize in sewing for the home. We hope to see local chapters started in cities

About the Authors

across the USA soon. For more information, write to them at the address in the Resource List, page 156.

Happy sewing and serging!

Pati Palmer
Pati Palmer

No matter what the style of your home, you can create wonderful rooms like the ones you'll see in this book. We started with these eight homes, ranging from an elaborate Georgian colonial to a simple ranch (and even a travel trailer, pg 134). In spite of the wide variety of styles, with careful evaluation, planning and inspiration, the results are truly wonderful!

Lynette Ranney Black is a Certified Kitchen Designer with six years of exerience in the kitchen and bath industry. Her design work can be seen in the kitchens and baths and many other rooms in her clients' homes. Lynette started her career as an Educational Representative for the regional distributor of a major line of sewing machines and sergers. She is the author of the best-selling Palmer/Pletsch Trends Bulletin, **"The Newest in Sewing Room Design"**. As Promotions Manager for Palmer/Pletsch, Lynette is responsible for the organization and promotion of their seminars and workshops held across the USA, Canada and Australia, as well as for their 4-day sewing workshops in Portland, Oregon. When not working, sewing or designing a new room, you'll find Lynette deeply involved in family life with husband Paul and daughters, Kelsey and Jessica. They live in the second home that she and Paul have completely remodelled.

Linda Wisner is Design Director for Palmer/Pletsch and the person responsible for the look of all Palmer/Pletsch books and printed materials. Her background in graphic, interior and landscape design (plus food styling) comes together in this book. In the 70s she worked in an interior design studio in St. Paul Minnesota, then as an illustrator, and later as graphic designer at Stretch & Sew. As owner of her own award-winning design studio and advertising agency, Linda began working with Palmer/Pletsch in 1980. During that time she also co-authored the *Instant Interiors* booklets with partner Gail Brown, designed a line of whimsical stuffed animal patterns for San Francisco Pattern Company, and worked with many other clients in the home sewing industry, including Metrosene. A move to Portland, Oregon, in 1987 brought her to Palmer/Pletsch, full-time, and to her current home which you'll see photographed throughout this book.

Welcome to the World of Do-It-Yourself Home Decorating—with Fabric and a Serger.

Your home should be a satisfying place. You should feel GOOD there. Our goal in this book is to help you make it happen.

The home decorating projects in this book are far from intimidating. Many start with fabric rectangles or squares sewn together with simple, straight seaming and finishing on the machine or serger. Whether they are simple or slightly more involved, we guide you through each project, highlighting where serging makes the project faster, easier, more durable, or more creative. We also highlight quick projects.

We decided the most exciting way to show you what was possible was to show you complete rooms, so this book is filled with rooms of all shapes, sizes and styles, starting with bedrooms and bathrooms and moving on through the house. To inspire you, we've done more than put sewing projects in a room. Each has been accessorized and the furniture arranged so it WORKS. The little details make the difference between stiff, uninviting spaces and comfortable, beautiful places you just can't resist!

So, we invite you to flip through these pages. Let yourself respond instinctively to what you see. Then stop and think about what you like, what attracts you. Notice the colors, the shapes, the textures, the lighting. All these things contribute to a mood, to

giving each room a personality. Some will match your personality. Some won't. YOUR home SHOULD match your (and your family's) personality. Have fun exploring that personality. From our photos, pick a room, a corner of a room, or just a pillow or a placemat, then make it your own.

Why a Serger?

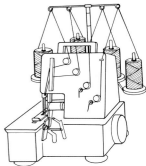

A serger trims, stitches and finishes a seam in one simple step.

Over the last few years we've discovered that the serger, in addition to being an ideal utilitarian companion to the sewing machine, has lots of creative potential for adding decorative touches to the garments we make.

We've spent months applying both the utilitarian and the creative possibilities to the home. With a serger you can simulate complicated hand or machine-sewn techniques, create decorative stitches possible only on the serger, **and** make items like tassels and piping in colors perfectly matched to your fabrics. No more endless searching for that non-existent ready-made product!

NOTE: Not all sergers can do all stitches. Become familiar with what **yours** can do. Team up with a friend to expand your options. OR, invest in a second serger! Just think how nice it would be to have one set for a rolled edge all the time! See "Serger Basics," beginning on page 142.

How to Use This Book

You will see a wide range of rooms and many different decorating styles in this book. You will also discover that although the results can differ dramatically, the actual techniques reappear over and over with minor variations.

That means that once you learn how to make Roman shades, you can easily make a cloud shade by adding just a few steps with very little additional effort!

Once you've made elegant serger piping with Decor 6 thread, like we did in Eleanor's Room on page 8, you can EASILY change threads, use a larger cord, adjust your tensions slightly, and create a whole different look for another room!

Because we wanted to show you as many projects as we could possibly fit into these pages, we have not always taken the space to repeat instructions for a technique that appears in another chapter. Instead you'll find a page reference.

In other cases we show you alternative ways to create the same thing. In one chapter you'll learn how to do something traditionally. In another, you'll learn how to use wonderful shortcuts and new products such as Gosling tapes (page 153). We've shown some pillows with removable covers that have zipper openings and others with zipperless, envelope openings (for those of you who hate zippers). If you've selected a specific project in a particular room but want to see what the construction alternatives are, check the Index on pages 157-158 and choose the one that works for you.

A Few Ground Rules...

For the most part we have not departed from the standard "rules" of sewing you learned "way back when." But keep a few things in mind:

1. Add 1/2" whenever directed to add seam allowances to a pattern, unless otherwise specified. This makes math calculations easier than the traditional 5/8" allowance.

2. If no seam allowances have been added and you are instructed to serge, let the serger knife barely skim the fabric edge to ensure nice, clean edges and perfect stitching.

3. There are no yardage charts in this book since every window, chair and room is different and fabric widths range from 45" to 120". Yardage requirements vary accordingly.

What we **have** tried to do is give you guidance on measuring and creating your own simple patterns for each project. On pages 150-151 you'll find guidelines for figuring yardage. Books and magazines often include approximate yardage charts. Collect them for your files. (Instant Interiors booklets are a good source. See page 155).

There are also excellent home decorating patterns available. McCall's Pattern Company features many exciting projects for those who like the security of a pattern with complete yardage and sewing how-tos. See the home dec and crafts pattern sections of the catalog.

The Reference Section

See **Serger Basics**, pages 142-148, for a refresher course on serging. It includes descriptions of many decorative threads and how to balance tensions, do flatlocking and create beautiful rolled edges, plus decorative stitch variations.

Home Decorating Basics explains decorating terms used in the book and includes basic techniques for using invaluable new home decorating aids, such as Quik Trak and Gosling tapes (page 153). Fabric selection, figuring yardage, and how to piece for larger projects are also covered.

On pages 155-156, the "Resource List" includes the sources for the beautiful fabrics and notions used in the finished rooms. It also includes a list of other publications with ideas for designing, planning and sewing projects for the home. For even more information on serging we highly recommend the other *Palmer/Pletsch* books on serging, **Sewing With Sergers, Creative Serging** and **The Serger Idea Book.** Also watch for *Palmer/Pletsch* seminars offered around the country in the spring and fall of each year, or ask your favorite fabric store to sponsor one!

The Final Goal

We hope this book provides you with the inspiration and the instruction you need to creatively transform your home into a warm and inviting place. Though we don't want your friends' reactions to your newly decorated room to be, *"Oh, I see you have a serger,"* with a serger you can create a room that **will** generate the response of *"Ohhhhh....how nice!"*

Eleanor's Room

Eleanor Roosevelt stayed in this room when visiting the original owners of this elegant, turn-of-the-century home in Portland, Oregon. Pati Palmer and her husband now own the home and named the room after its famous occupant. They even commissioned local architect/artist Gary Reddick to create the portrait of Eleanor that hangs in this historic room which still functions as a guest room for the couple's frequent out-of-town visitors.

We created this magical space from a nearly empty room, drawing inspiration from the brass bed, heirloom coverlet and colorful Italian lamps. We had envisioned a pure white room with lots of heirloom serging/sewing. But then we found the beautiful, pastel Waverly print and the room just evolved around it—a lesson that it is **OK** to change your mind along the way! Be open to new possibilities as they come along and let them steer you in new directions.

> **PRO TIP:** When selecting paint for walls, buy a quart and try a large area before committing to the whole thing. The color might surprise you when you see more than a tiny swatch.

1. *Window draping with Decor 6 rolled edges.*
2. *QUICK gathered sheers with simple rolled edges, plus SUPER QUICK, simple lace hanging from Lace Country with side edges finished with rolled edges.*
3. *Fine linen top cloths with serger fagotting borders.*
4. *QUICK napkins finished with Decor 6 rolled edge.*
5. *SIMPLE oval and round tablecloths finished with Decor 6 rolled edges.*
6. *Dinette chairs transformed with padding and slipcovers with double row of Decor 6 serger piping and Decor 6 rolled edges.*
7. *Canopy of wide sheers with QUICK rolled-edge finish.*

8. Heirloom serging on linen pillow covers mingled with antique ones.
9. Double-ruffle dust ruffle from Waverly print with Decor 6 rolled edges.
10. Rocking chair cushion with Decor 6 piping.
11. Designer towels with lace and serged trim.

1. Window Drapes

Triple window treatments don't look crowded at Eleanor's windows because we extended the wooden poles 15" beyond the window on each side. That way the side drapes don't block out any of the wonderful light or hide the beautiful lace and sheers.

For the side drapes, we cut a length of 60"-wide fabric in half lengthwise, then with **wrong sides together**, we serged a lining to each panel with rolled edges of Decor 6. (See page 148 for rolled edges.) Panels are shirred onto wooden poles through a top casing.

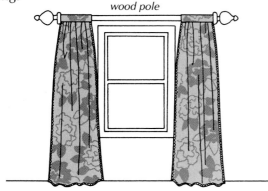

wood pole

The top swag was added separately for ease. (We tried making the sides and top as one piece, but the draping challenge drove us crazy—something you don't need!) To determine size:

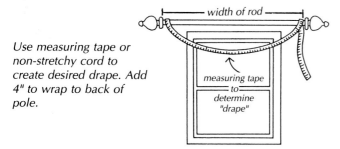

width of rod

Use measuring tape or non-stretchy cord to create desired drape. Add 4" to wrap to back of pole.

measuring tape to determine "drape"

Cut fabric and lining pieces with top edge equal to width of rod; bottom edge the desired drape plus 4". Use a half-width of 60" fabric.

width of rod

TOP
BOTTOM
30"

width of "drape" + 4"

Place fabric and lining, **wrong sides together**, and roll-edge finish using decorative thread.

To mount, use staple gun (an electric one is REALLY handy!), a ladder and a friend. Gather one slanted edge together until folds look good. Roll rod forward so top of rod is facing you and you can see

what you are doing. Staple in place to secure. (This is why we used **wooden** poles.) Repeat at other end, with friend guiding you so gathers match on left and right sides. Staple fabric at intervals along the top of the rod to finish.

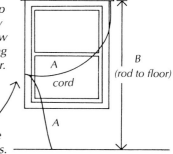

(Unfortunately, this **will** have to be redone after each cleaning! With regular vacuuming, however, complete cleaning should not be needed very often.)

2. Window Coverings

The combination of lace and sheers is a very romantic touch. And **very** easy! We cut lace panels from Lace Country to the width of the window and finished the sides with a rolled edge. The panels slide onto the inside rod of a double curtain rod.

Make two panels of sheers for each window, cut and pieced to equal three times the width of the window. To determine length:

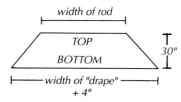

Let a long length of cord drop from rod at center of window and puddle on the floor. Draw up to desired drape. Cut string where it just brushes the floor. This is the length of one side of each sheer panel (A). Add 4" for casing allowance.

A
cord
B (rod to floor)
A

Mark point on window frame where rosette will hold sheers.

The length of the opposite side of each panel is equal to the distance from rod to floor (B) + 4"-deep casing allowance. One panel should be the mirror image of the other. Each should be 3 times the window width.

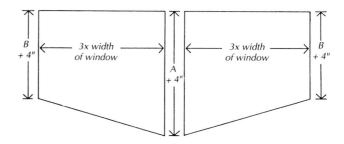

B + 4" *3x width of window* *A + 4"* *3x width of window* *B + 4"*

1. Cut panels from sheers.

2. Serge a rolled edge with plain white thread to finish any raw edges on sides and bottom. If piecing, use rolled edge to seam. Test stitch length and width, first.

3. Sandwich two panels together with long sides opposite. Roll-edge seam both layers together at top, then fold down to form casing large enough to allow rod to slip through easily. Topstitch to form casing.

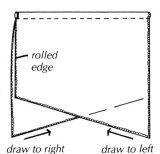

rolled edge

draw to right   draw to left

4. Hang sheers on outside rod of a double curtain rod. Screw cup hooks into woodwork or wall at point marked earlier for rosette placement. Draw each sheer layer to opposite side of window with 10"-12" cord and tie to cup hook.

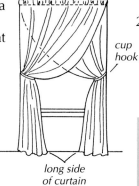

cup hook

long side of curtain

Make Rosettes

These, too, are simple and beautiful. For each rosette cut an 8"x 48" strip of sheer fabric. Roll-edge finish both long edges with stitch length set at 4mm.

Fold strip in half lengthwise and baste along fold. Draw up basting to gather and hand roll strip to create rose shape. Hand sew securely to finish.

Mount rosettes at cup hooks by hooking a thread loop over hook.

3. Fagotted Linen Table Toppers

With the serger you can easily duplicate the look of heirloom fagotting—but do it on the straight of grain only! First cut linen squares to desired size, **minus** 5".

Then cut 4"-wide strips of linen to the length of each side plus 7". To fagot:

1. Press under ½" on edges of square and on one long edge of each strip.

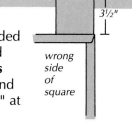

fold under ½"

2. Set serger for flatlocking with Decor 6, size 14/90 needle and nylon monofilament thread in **both** loopers. Use widest stitch width; test to find best stitch length. The longer the stitch, the more open the fagotting. Loosen needle tension (very loose) and tighten lower looper tension.

PRO TIP: If using Decor 6, watch its feeding off the spool, especially when it is nearing empty. To eliminate stitching hangups, reel off some thread by hand as you stitch (reel off, stitch, reel off, etc.).

3. Working on one side of square at a time, align folded edge of a strip with folded edge of square, **right sides together**, letting strip extend beyond side of square 3½" at each end.

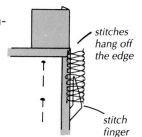

3½"

wrong side of square

4. Guiding folded edges together, flatlock **slowly**, with needle barely entering the folds. (Stitches hang off the edge.) Repeat for each side, letting ends of strips extend from square.

stitches hang off the edge

stitch finger

5. Open fabric and pull layers apart to reveal fagotting. Anchor each side by stitching on **right side** with conventional machine using a decorative or satin stitch and pulling fabric flat as you stitch. From underside, trim away seam allowance close to stitching.

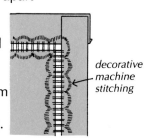

decorative machine stitching

PRO TIP: Use a pin-tuck foot for smoother traveling over the satin stitches. To create a prettier satin stitch on conventional machine, slightly loosen needle tension (or tighten bobbin tension). Cotton or rayon machine embroidery thread gives a nice sheen.

To finish corners and edges:

Miter corners: Fold cloth diagonally, **right sides together**, so two adjacent sides line up as shown. Mark diagonal on strips with vanishing marker, pin and sew. Trim seam allowances to ¼". Serge over first stitching with rolled edge. Press.

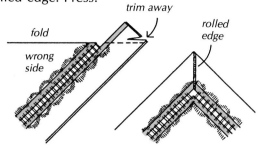

To hem, roll-edge finish with white thread along ½" seam line, turning corners or serging off the ends. Secure serger tails (page 143).

The top cloth on the small table by the wicker rocker was made in the same way.

4. Simple Napkins

Making napkins couldn't be simpler! Cut squares of napkin fabric and finish with a rolled edge using Decor 6 in upper looper. (See page 144 for turning corners.)

5. Round and Oval Tablecloths

Finishing round and oval tablecloths is as simple as the napkins. Measuring and cutting is the tricky part.

Measuring and Cutting a Circle

1. Measure diameter of top and add 2 drops.

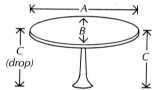

2. Cut square of fabric to determined dimensions. If piecing is necessary, see page 150.

3. Fold square in half, then in half again.

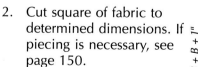

4. Tie a marking pen to a non-stretchy cord the length of one side of the square. Pin other end of cord at center. Draw an arc from corner to corner.

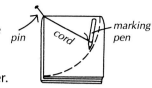

5. Cut along arc to create circle.

Measuring and Cutting an Oval

This works best if you make a template of the table top. Use an old sheet, or large sheets of paper taped together. Lay across the table top. Trace and cut out the shape. Measure the length (A) and the width (B). To each measurement, add the two drops to floor (C).

Measure and cut a rectangle to the determined dimensions. If piecing is necessary, see page 150. Place template in center. With yardstick, carefully mark edge of oval every 6"-8". Connect the dots and cut it out!

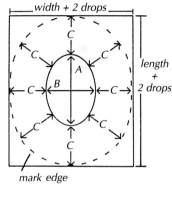

Both cloths were finished with a rolled-edge hem using Decor 6 in the upper looper. Because you have cut the fabric just to the floor, barely skim the fabric with the knife as you serge.

6. The Chairs

These chairs started life as aluminum dinette chairs with plastic covers. A little padding and a slipcover did wonders! We designed the covers, but hired a professional seamstress to make the slipcovers, providing her with the serger piping used in a double row around the top of the skirt. (For slipcover how-tos, see the Resource List, page 155.)

The bottom edge of the skirt is finished with Decor 6 rolled edges. An underskirt of Lace Country lace and the fat shirred piping along the top edge are pretty details. (See page 25 for shirred piping how-tos). A double row of serger piping is set between chair seat and skirt (see page 148 for serger piping).

7. Sheer Canopy and Ring

Yards and yards of sheers are needed for this lush, romantic look. Allow for at least 25 yards of the widest fabric you can find. Then have fun. The selvages can be left as is, or finish them with rolled edges.

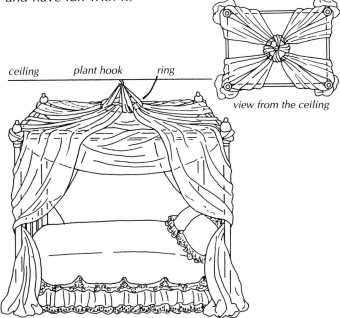

The draping swoops from a plant hook in the ceiling and around a fat fabric ring. For the ring, make three 3'-4' long, fat tubes of fabric and stuff with polyester fiberfill. Twist them around an embroidery hoop and hand sew together, tucking open ends to inside.

Now take four lengths of sheer, each long enough to go up one post, then from one corner of the bed diagonally across to the other and down to swoop and puddle generously on the floor. Additional lengths of sheer were draped like swags along each side and the foot, with ends wrapping around the brass posts. The illustrations below show approximately how we put it all together, but we have to emphasize that it is a trial and error process. We pulled this way and that until it looked right. Take off your shoes, climb on the bed, and have fun with it!

ceiling   plant hook   ring

view from the ceiling

opening for light

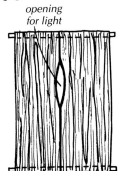

At the head of the bed, sheer fabric was shirred onto two rods mounted on the wall. Use at least 3 times the finished width. Make casings top and bottom. We pieced ours so piecing seam came directly up middle, leaving an opening for the light sconce to poke through.

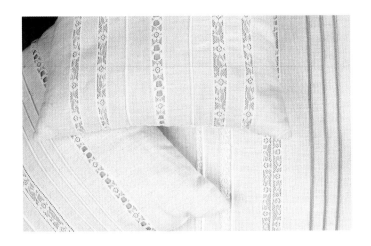

8. Pillows with Heirloom Serging

We enhanced the antique coverlet and pillow shams with "new" heirloom pillows created on the serger. We started with linen squares cut larger than the finished pillow size so we could make serger pin tucks (page 70) and add lace insertion. The removable covers were constructed with zipperless backs like the pillow shams in Kelsey's room, page 54. For additional heirloom serging ideas, see the nursery on page 69.

9. Double-Ruffle Dust Ruffle

We've repeated the fabric-plus-lace theme here to create a pretty, double ruffle.

1. **Measure:** (You'll need to remove the mattress to get down to the box spring for accurate measuring.)

```
  __ width (A)
+ __ length (B)
+ __ length (B)
= __ ×2½ = ____
```

This is the length of the fabric strip and the lace strip. Determine measurement of fabric ruffle drop by how much lace you want to show. Hold strips up to bed to determine best effect. Measure and add 1" for top seam allowance. Add 1" top seam allowance to lace. Cut and piece strips as necessary.

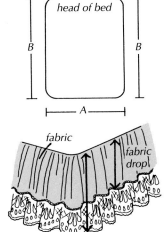

head of bed

B   B

A

fabric

fabric drop

lace drop

2. Finish one long edge of fabric strip with a rolled edge, using Decor 6, and just skimming edge.

3. Now, use a wonderful product we have discovered, Gosling Tape (Resource List, page 155). This

line of innovative tapes make gathering, shirring, smocking and pleating a breeze. (For additional information on these tapes, see page 153.) We used a length of the 2-Cord Shirring Tape to fit the full length of ruffle strip.

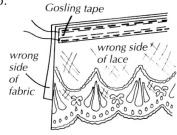

Gosling tape

4. Align top edges of fabric and lace. Pin 2-Cord Shirring Tape on wrong side of lace, even with top edge. Machine baste along top and bottom edges.

wrong side of fabric • *wrong side of lace*

5. For dust ruffle platform, cut a fabric rectangle to fit box spring, adding 1" at each edge for seams. Use a sheet or inexpensive fabric since it won't show when dust ruffle is finished.

> **QUICK TIP:** Since you probably don't have a cutting board big enough for this, lay fabric on top of box spring and cut to size. Remember to add the seam allowances!

6. At one short edge of platform, press under ½", then another ½" and topstitch hem in place.

7. Now, to position ruffle for gathering, count how many pieced strips make up the ruffle strip. Take the total measurement of the sides and bottom end of the bed (step 1) and divide by the number of strips. Mark off sections on platform with pins. Match pins with piecing seams of strip, **right sides together**. Knot cords together and pull to gather ruffle to fit. Pin in place.

(A+B+B) ÷ number of strips = ___" (C)

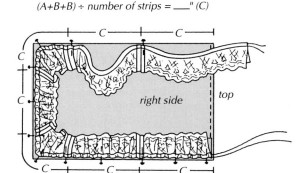

right side *top*

8. Stitch ruffle layers to rectangle, using 1" seam allowances. **Do not** catch Gosling tape in the stitching. Pull out machine basting to remove tape and save it for other gathering projects. (You'll find it **very** handy to have one hand).

Smooth the completed dust ruffle over the box spring and replace the mattress.

10. Rocking Chair Cushion

The white wicker rocker sits invitingly near the window with a "squishy" cushion for added comfort. For laundering ease, we made an inner cushion cover of muslin and a removable cover from printed fabric.

1. Cut 2"-thick foam to exact dimensions of chair seat. Wrap in a layer of quilt batting to "soften" edges and secure with **long** hand basting stitches.

2. Measure padded foam (page 154) to determine size of muslin cover, adding ½" all around for seam allowance. Cut two pieces of muslin to size.

3. Stitch muslin pieces, **right sides together**, leaving an opening for inserting foam cushion. Insert cushion and hand sew opening closed.

4. Cut printed cover top same size as muslin. Make pattern for bottom as shown and cut two bottom pieces.

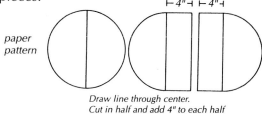

paper pattern

Draw line through center.
Cut in half and add 4" to each half

5. Serge straight edges, or press under ¼" and edgestitch. Press under 2" on one piece and 1" on other; machine baste in place as shown. Overlap bottom pieces on cushion cover top, **wrong sides together**. Machine baste ½" from outer edges.

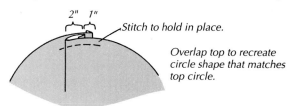

Stitch to hold in place.

Overlap top to recreate circle shape that matches top circle.

6. With Decor 6 in upper looper, serge using rolled edge stitch, with serger needle on top of basting.

> **PRO TIP:** To begin serging a circle, cut away a 2" section of seam allowance; begin and end stitching in the cut-away area. Also see page 145.
>
> *seamline*

7. Insert muslin pillow, and you're done!

11. Designer Towels (See page 21).

12. The Dressing Table

Look "under the covers" here and you will find secondhand furniture...and why not?! The dressing table is an old table with plywood cut the desired size and topped with plate glass with rounded edges. The stool was a $3 find that we had slipcovered to match the chairs. The mirror was on sale in an antique shop.

The dressing table "petticoat" is a flat panel of the Waverly print, open at the center for knee room.

1. Measure around table side to center front (A) and from tabletop to floor (B). Cut two panels to this size, adding 1" to width and 3" to height.

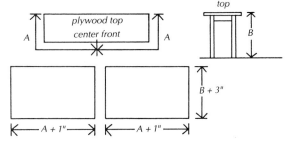

2. Serge a rolled-edge hem along sides and bottom of each panel, trimming ½".

3. Using a staple gun, staple panel to top of plywood, keeping hem edge even with floor.

4. Cut two linen panels 3 times the width of the fabric panels and 1" deeper. Cut a 4½" strip off bottom of each panel and re-attach with serger fagoting (page 12). Serge a rolled-edge hem along sides and bottom of each panel.

5. Stitch Gosling Shirring Tape along top edge of each panel. Staple to plywood at back corners and center front. Knot cords together and pull to gather evenly, stapling in place along top around edge of plywood and over stapled flat fabric panels.

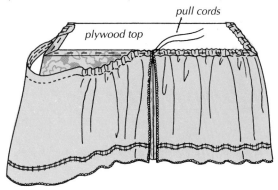

6. For draping, roll-edge finish two short ends of a length of sheer fabric cut the measurement around table **plus** enough length for 6 drops and 30" extra for "swoops."

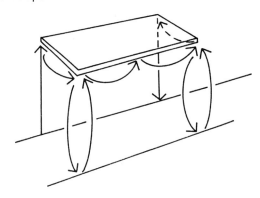

Beginning at one back corner, staple fabric to plywood at corners, then arrange swoops and staple. Make rosettes (page 12) and hand-sew to draping in locations shown in photo.

7. Cut a piece of printed fabric and a piece of linen the size of plywood top. Press; spread smoothly on plywood. Cover with glass. (We did not finish raw edges since the fabric must match glass size **exactly**.

13. Shirred Mirror Frame

We created this mirror by shirring fabric over a frame cut from foam-center board (Foamcore) available at art supply shops.

1. Trace shape of mirror onto Foamcore board.

2. For a 4½"-wide frame, carefully mark 4" outside of mirror line and ½" **inside** of line. Use a **sharp** X-acto or utility knife to cut frame from the foam board. (Protect your cutting surface!)

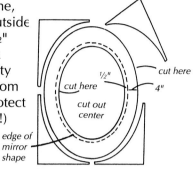

3. Cut a second foamcore oval 1" smaller than the outside dimensions of the first.

4. Cut an 11"-wide strip of fabric 5 times the circumference of the oval, piecing as necessary. Zigzag over a **heavy** cord along each edge.

5. Draw cord to tightly gather one edge and wrap around inside edge of foamcore frame. Use staple gun or pins to anchor in place.

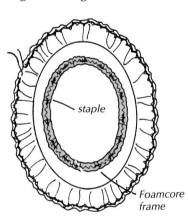

6. Draw up outside gathering cord. Smoothing gathers as you go, bring fabric over front of frame and around to back. Push pins through fabric into Foamcore to hold in place. Thread a sturdy needle with topstitching thread and sew securely together at back. Remove pins.

7. Lay fabric-covered frame face down, and mirror face down on top of it, centering carefully. Using a hot glue gun, apply glue generously (and carefully!) to back of fabric-covered frame, and **immediately** press foamcore backing into place.

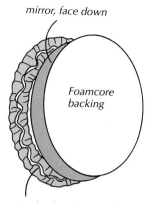

Apply glue. Center mirror and Foamcore backing over frame.

Note: Our mirror had a wooden backing. We were able to mount screw eyes through the Foamcore and into wood, then twist wire through for hanging. This also anchored the mirror to the frame. For a mirror without a backing, in Step 6 above, apply glue to mirror back as well as frame before applying foam board backing. (There **is** a risk of damaging "silver" backing with glue.)

Mirror can then be mounted by nailing or screwing through Foamcore frame into wall, hiding nail or screw heads in fabric folds.

14. The Accessories

It's often little flourishes that finish a room. Eleanor's dressing table wouldn't be quite so pretty without its array of covered boxes, bags of potpourri and the special jewelry keeper, all tucked among treasured family photos. We used Decor 6 for all decorative accent stitching.

Potpourri Bags

Sweetly scented potpourri bags are easy to make on the serger and add a lovely aroma to any room. We stacked and tied several with wide satin ribbon. Another goes solo with pretty rolled-edge pin tucks.

For each small bag to stack:

Roll-edge seam two 4½"x 6½" fabric pieces together on three sides. Add your favorite potpourri and roll-edge seam the opening edges together.

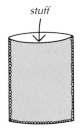

stuff

For the embellished bag:

front

back   *pintucks*

1. Make three rolled-edge pin tucks (page 70) down the center of a 6"x 10½" piece of fabric for bag front. Cut a bag back to match size of completed bag front. Serge, **right sides together**.

2. Finish top edge with narrow ruffled lace, serger piping and a 2"-wide bias strip of self-fabric as shown. (Finish one long edge of strip with rolled edge, first.) Add potpourri and tie with a 1"-wide satin ribbon.

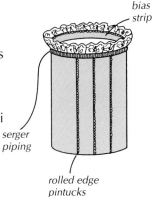

bias strip

serger piping

rolled edge pintucks

Jewelry Keeper

Tuck earrings and rings into the central compartments and chains and beads in the center of this pretty case. It can double as a traveling case, too.

1. Cut 7½" and 12"-diameter circles from a print and from a solid. (Use silvercloth for solid color to protect jewelry from tarnish.) Serge each set of circles, **wrong sides together**, using a balanced stitch with Decor 6 in the upper and lower loopers, if your machine can handle it.

7½"

12"

2. Stitch ½"-wide gathered lace to ½"-wide eyelet trim. Stitch to print side of larger circle, 1" in from outer edge. Thread ribbon through eyelet leaving 3"-long tails.

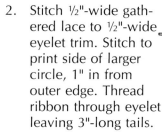

ribbon   *print fabric*

1"

3. Center and pin smaller circle on larger circle with solid sides facing. Stitch 3"-diameter circle through all layers, **leaving an opening**.

Stuff with polyester fiberfill to create the "base." Stitch opening closed. Stitch 8 diagonal lines through all layers as shown.

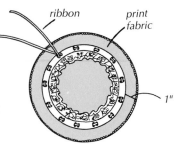

stuff in here, then stitch closed

stitch diagonal lines through all layers

solid

print

Covered Boxes

We covered a set of purchased boxes with fabric using transfer web (page 64). Then we glued on lace, rolled-edge chain and serger piping trims (page 148).

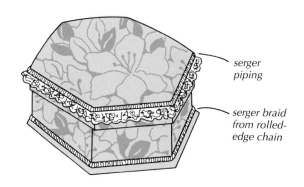

serger piping

serger braid from rolled-edge chain

Eleanor's Bath

It probably didn't look like this in Eleanor's day, but we don't know a woman who wouldn't enjoy luxuriating in this elegant and romantically feminine bath. Clouds of fabric surround the tub in our shower curtain adaptation of a cloud shade. We love the pink glow created with sponge-painted walls and ceiling.

1. Cloud Shower Curtain

1. Cut curtain panel 2½ x the desired finished width across tub opening and 1½ times desired finished length. Piece as needed for the width (page 150). Finish sides and top edge with serging.

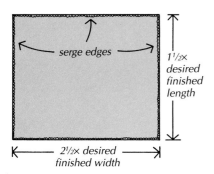

serge edges

1½× desired finished length

2½× desired finished width

2. Press under 1" on each side of curtain. Stitch. Press under 4" at top; pin 3-Cord Shirring Tape in place ¼" below upper edge. Stitch above and below each cord.

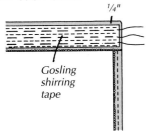

¼"

Gosling shirring tape

3. Cut a 2½"-wide bottom facing and a piece of 6"-wide flat lace the width of the finished curtain panel plus 1". Finish all short ends with a ¼"-wide double hem or serge, trimming off ½" at each end. Serge finish one long edge of facing.

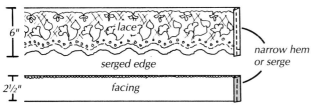

6" lace

serged edge

narrow hem or serge

2½" facing

4. **Right sides together**, stitch facing to bottom of curtain panel with lace sandwiched between. Press facing toward curtain and edgestitch through all

layers. Stitch again ¾" and 1½" from finished bottom edge. Insert a curtain weight strip.

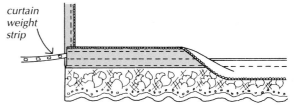

curtain weight strip

5. Hand sew or zigzag stitch draw cord rings in place as shown, placing one at top edge of bottom facing and ¾" in from edge on both sides. Place another approximately 34" from top finished edge. Sew Gosling Loop Tape between rings. Space additional rows of rings and loop tape approximately 24" apart across finished curtain.

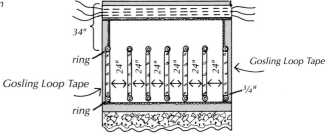

34"

ring

Gosling Loop Tape

24" 24" 24" 24" 24" 24"

Gosling Loop Tape

¾"

ring

6. Draw up top edge of shower curtain to match width of plastic curtain liner. Tie off cords and stitch over cord ends to anchor securely. Sew rings for shower hooks in line with holes for hooks in plastic liner. Hang curtain on shower curtain rod.

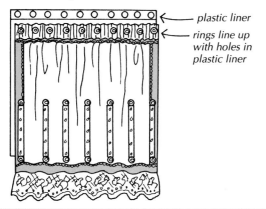

plastic liner

rings line up with holes in plastic liner

PRO TIP: Because of the width of the shower curtain, we pulled the shirring tape cords from both ends, gathering from the outside to the center and adjusting fullness evenly.

7. Tie non-stretchy cord (available from Gosling tapes, page 153) to each bottom ring and knot securely. Draw up cord evenly to desired length, knotting cord to each loop in loop tape as you go. Knot cord securely to upper ring and cut off excess cord.

PRO TIP: To make sure drawing and tying is evenly spaced so the poufs don't fall into one big puddle at the bottom of the curtain, first determine distance from top ring to floor (A). Measure curtain from top ring to bottom edge of lace (B). Subtract A from B and divide by **number of loops in the loop tape.** This is the amount of fabric that must be drawn up and tied off from loop to loop so poufs hang evenly and curtain clears the floor. You may have to experiment a little!

For example if your answer is 6, mark cord approximately every 6" so you know where to anchor it to loop tape loops as you draw it through. You may have to experiment a little!

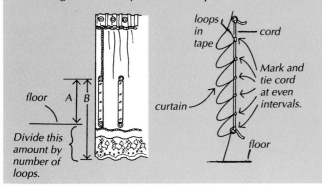

floor | A | B

Divide this amount by number of loops.

loops in tape

cord

Mark and tie cord at even intervals.

curtain

floor

2. Cloud Window Shade

1. Cut fabric twice the window width and 1½ times the length. Complete shade construction following steps 2,3 and 4 for shower curtain, above. Substitute a 3/8" metal dowel for drapery weight tape when hanging completed shade.

2. Hand sew or zigzag stitch draw cord rings in place, with one at top edge of bottom facing, ¾" in from edge on both sides. Place another ring just below shirring tape. Sew Gosling loop tape between rings and space rows of rings and tape about 18" apart.

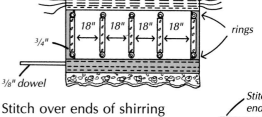

18" 18" 18" 18"

rings

¾"

3/8" dowel

3. Stitch over ends of shirring cords at **one** edge of shade, using a short stitch length and backstitching to secure. Pull on remaining cord ends to gather shade to desired width, **allowing enough width so shade wraps around ends of mounting board.**

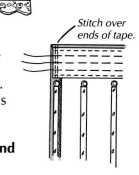

Stitch over ends of tape.

4. Stitch a 3"-wide strip of fabric to top edge of shade for mounting, stitching at top stitching line for shirring tape. String as shown on page 33, tying cords securely to bottom rings.

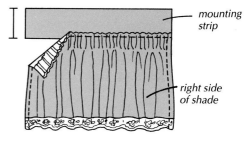

mounting strip

right side of shade

5. Cut a piece of 1"x 2" common lumber to the desired width and cover with fabric. Staple shade to mounting board (page 34), wrapping shade around to cover ends of board.

6. Position screw eyes in board in line with rows of rings and loops. (See page 34). Install above window frame with angle irons.

board

angle iron

window frame

shade

wall

CROSS SECTION

7. String shade through the screw eyes as shown on page 34.

8. Screw an awning cleat to woodwork or wall to hold cords when shade is drawn.

3. Hamper Cover

We made a removable cover with lace and serger piping trim (page 148) for the removable lid of the whitewashed wicker hamper. We created a fabric envelope that fit comfortably over the lid, making it large enough to accommodate two layers of polyester fleece padding that we stapled to the lid.

1. To determine how large to cut the envelope front and back pieces, measure the lid with the desired padding already stapled in place. Add seam allowances all around and an extra 5" at one long edge of the front piece for the envelope flap.

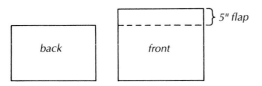

2. Finish one long edge of envelope back with serging.

3. Machine baste serger piping and wide gathered lace to envelope front, beginning and ending 5" from one long edge as shown. **With right sides together**, stitch envelope front to back. Turn right side out.

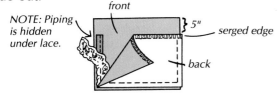

4. Press under a narrow, doubled hem at short ends of flap. Stitch. Press under ¼", then 1" on remaining long edge. Position and stitch loop half of Velcro hook and loop tape at inner folded edge.

5. Slip lid into envelope and mark position for remaining half of Velcro. Remove and apply remaining half of Velcro to right side of envelope back.

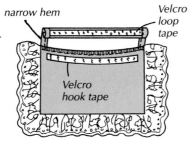

4. Designer Towels

Cotton lace and fabric bands finished with rolled edges made easy work of creating designer linens for the bath. We used the woven-in bands on the towels as a guide for positioning wide gathered lace under the fabric band, then topstitched band in place next to the rolled edges.

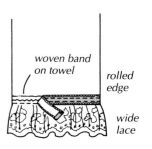

Washcloths and Finger Towels

We cut 12"-square washcloths from an extra towel to eliminate woven borders. We finished them with rolled edges, curving corners as we stitched. We added gathered lace, placing it under the rolled edge and stitching alongside. The finishing touch is a rose motif cut from extra lace and stitched in place with the serpentine zigzag stitch on a conventional machine.

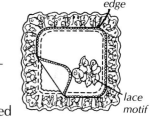

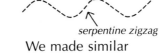

serpentine zigzag

We made similar 8½"x13" finger towels with rolled edges and the same design embellishments.

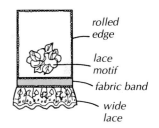

21

Across the Hall...

Pati chose this spacious room for the master bedroom. The room was transformed from the sterile, all-white "before" shown below to this elaborate retreat with yards and yards of coordinating prints and solids from Springs. Now it's a cozy place to read and relax before retiring.

We upholstered the walls with fabric over batting and Quik Trak, an exciting new product that attaches fabric to walls. (How-tos on page 28.) Ann Person of Stretch & Sew tied everything together with her special gift, this painting of a lively floral bouquet that reveals yet another facet of her creative genius.

1. Traditional slipcovers.
2. Balloon shade.
3. Swag and drape roll-edge finished with Decor 6.
4. Comforter using new 90"-wide fabric from Springs.
5. Sheets from 90"-wide fabric with decorative rolled-edge seams in Decor 6 thread.
6. Pillows and pillow shams with shirred piping trim.
7. Double-ruffle dust ruffle hemmed with rolled edge using Decor 6.
8. Quik Trak-upholstered walls padded with Hobbs batting.

1. Slipcovers

Unless you are truly ambitious, find a skilled professional to make fitted slipcovers for you. (See the Resource List, page 155.) Then you'll have more time to focus your creativity on the rest of the room!

2. Balloon Shade

We love the full look of festooned Austrian shades, but we wanted a window covering that looked beautiful whether up or down. We decided on this balloon shade adaptation with a gathered top. Basic construction is similar to Roman shades, page 33.

1. Cut fabric and lining, piecing if needed (page 150).Remember that the new 90" wide fabrics like these from Springs make most piecing unnecessary!

   Width = 2½x inside window measurement
   Length = inside window height + 30" (so it's pouffy, even when lowered)

2. With fabric and lining **wrong sides together**, roll-edge finish all around.

3. Stitch Gosling Loop Tape in place, spacing rows of tape **no more than 12" apart.** (See Gosling Tape information on page 153.)

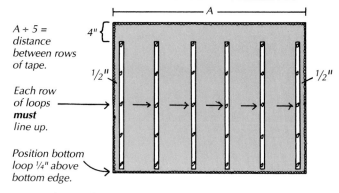

A ÷ 5 = distance between rows of tape.

Each row of loops **must** line up.

Position bottom loop ¼" above bottom edge.

4. Stitch Gosling 2-Cord Shirring Tape across top of shade.

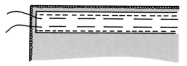

5. Tie cords together at each end, then pull to gather to desired finished width (inside dimension of window). Secure cords.

6. String cords through loops in tape and mount as shown for Roman shades on page 34.

3. Swag and Tails

For unity, we chose to frame the windows with the same fabric used to cover the walls. This classical treatment is really three elements—a top swag and two separate side "tails" stapled to a cornice board mounted over the window. As in Eleanor's room (page 8), this framing extends 10" **beyond** each side of the windows to let in more light, allow the balloon shades to show, and to create a more dramatic effect.

Start with these basic shapes:

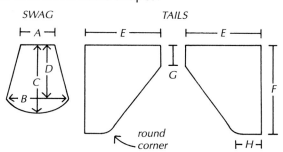

SWAG

TAILS

A = finished width across top of window
B = 1½x finished width
C = 2½x finished depth
D = ¾ of C

E = 2½x finished width
F = height from cornice board to floor + 2"
G = ⅕ of F (10-18")
H = ½ of E

Yes, we know this looks intimidating, but just take one element at a time, and it will all come together!

1. Make a pattern for each piece, then cut out fabric and lining, remembering to flip pattern for right and left tail. We lined the striped fabric with the fabric used for the balloon shades.

> **PRO TIP:** Swags are traditionally cut on the bias for better drapability. Because we wanted the stripes to run horizontally, we cut ours on straight of grain.

2. With fabric and lining **wrong sides together**, finish all edges with a rolled edge in a decorative thread.

3. Easestitch across top of each tail.

To drape:

This is a "sculptural" process, with no hard and fast rules. You will need push pins, staple gun, and a 1"x4" cornice board cut to the desired finished swag width. (We extended the cornice board 10" beyond each side of the window.) Wrap the board with a piece of fabric and staple in place.

1. Place board along the edge of a counter or table so you can work with fabric hanging down.

2. Begin with the tails. Draw up easestitching to partially gather. Create three 4"-deep pleats along inside, then adjust gathers to achieve final fit. Use pushpins to temporarily hold in place.

Wrap around corner to cover end of board.

Wrap fabric over top of board 1½" to 2", and staple pleats and gathers in place.

board

pushpins

3. Staple top edge of swag to top of board from center out, stopping 15" from each end. At each end, hand gather remaining fabric and staple in place at top of board as shown.

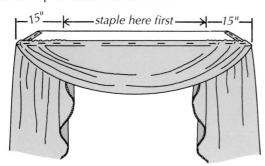

|←15"→|←— staple here first —→|←15"→|

4. Mount cornice board as shown on page 31.

4. Comforter

This generous bed deserved a generously stuffed comforter. We finished it with plump shirred piping.

1. Measure bed.

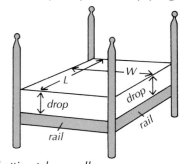

rail   *rail*

Comforter width =
W + 2 drops + 1" + ___" batting take-up allowance

Comforter length =
L + 1 drop + 1" + ___" batting take-up allowance

See page 154 for measuring batting take-up allowance.

2. Cut top, lining and batting, piecing as necessary. With 90"-wide fabric, only a king-size comforter needs piecing. (See page 150).

Make shirred piping:

3. Cut fabric strips on bias or crossgrain, making them wide enough to wrap around chosen cording, **plus 1"**. Piece into one long strip 2½-3 times the length around sides and bottom edge of comforter.

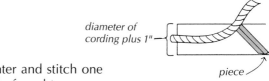

diameter of cording plus 1"

piece

4. Center and stitch one end of cord to **wrong side** of strip. Wrap strip around cord with raw edges even. Machine baste for 6" using zipper foot to get close to cord **without crowding it**. Stop in needle down position.

5. Raise presser foot and push stitched part of strip along cord behind needle until fabric is as loosely or tightly shirred as desired. Continue stitching and shirring. Stitch across end to secure.

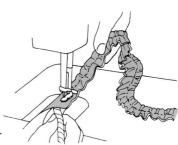

5. Custom Sheets

We just couldn't find sheets we liked for this oversized bed with its extra-thick mattress, so we made our own from Springs 90"-wide fabric!

For fitted bottom sheet:

1. Measure mattress. Add 1" seam allowances and 3" "tuck-under" allowance to all sides.

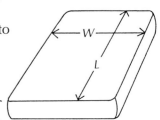

Bottom sheet width =
W + (depth x 2) + 2" seam allowance + 6" tuck-under

Bottom sheet length =
L + (depth x 2) + 2" seam allowance + 6" tuck-under

2. Cut out sheet. Piece as necessary. (See page 150).

3. Round corners using a plate or bowl as a pattern.

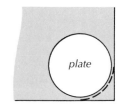

4. Serge raw edges or turn under ¼" and topstitch. Turn under ¾" and press.

5. Starting 6" in from each rounded corner, stitch around corner 5/8" in from fold.

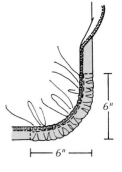

Thread ½"-wide elastic through each corner casing, draw up and secure ends with machine stitching.

6. Machine stitch hems on all sides to finish.

> **NOTE:** We made a second fitted sheet for the box spring because so much of it showed above the side rails.

> **NOTE:** For an alternate fitted sheet technique with mitered corners, see the crib sheet on page 71.

6. Machine baste piping to comforter fabric with raw edges even, using zipper foot to stitch close to cord. Machine baste quilt batting to lining. Stitch comforter to lining, **right sides together**, leaving top end open for turning.

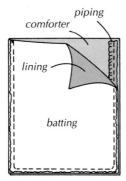

7. Turn comforter right side out and topstitch or hand slipstitch opening closed.

8. Secure all layers by "tufting" at evenly spaced intervals (6"-8" apart) across length and width of finished comforter.

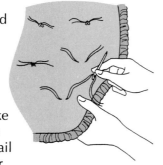

To tuft: Thread needle with crochet thread. Take a ¼"-long stitch through all layers, leaving a 4" tail at both ends of stitch for tying. Tie a square knot to secure "tuft."

For top sheet:

The band on the top sheet was made from the same floral as the comforter and roll-edge seamed to the sheet using Decor 6.

1. Cut and piece top sheet to same width as bottom sheet, and to the following length:

   __ *(mattress length)*
   + __ *(mattress depth)*
   + _7"_ *(1" seam allowance and 6" tuck-in)*
   = __ *Sheet length*

2. Cut 9"-wide strip of floral fabric to match width of sheet. Fold in half lengthwise, **wrong sides together**.

3. **On wrong side** of sheet, line up long raw edges of band with top edge of sheet. Serge through all three layers with rolled-edge stitching, using Decor 6 or other decorative thread in upper looper.

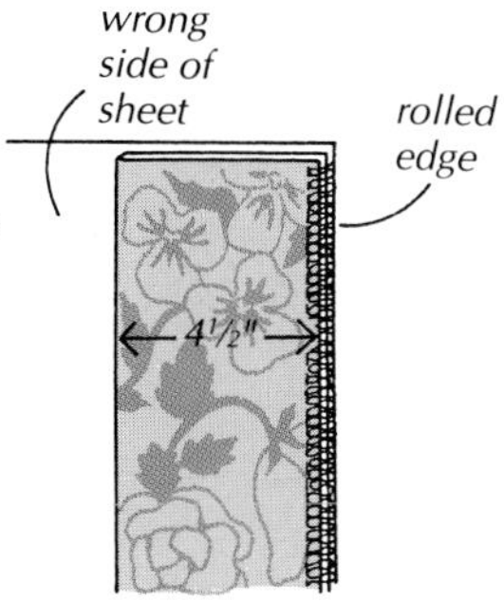

wrong side of sheet
rolled edge
4½"

4. Pull seam open so band is flat and rolled edge shows on **right side** of sheet.

5. Roll-edge finish raw edges on sides and bottom.

6. Pillows and Pillow Shams

Our pillow shams and round pillow have shirred piping that's not quite as fat as that on the comforter. Choose smaller cording and follow the shirring instructions on page 25. For complete pillow sham instructions, see page 53 (Kelsey's Room).

The shams fit standard bed pillows and we made three for this king size bed. The 16"-round pillow uses a Hobbs pillow form. The striped pillow matches the love seat cushions.

7. Dust Ruffle

Our double-ruffle dust ruffle combines two color-coordinated Springs fabrics. The bottom edges are finished with a Decor 6 rolled edge. Sides and bed end are separate pieces. Gosling 2-Cord Shirring Tape made the job a breeze.

The ruffle is mounted with Velcro hook and loop tape applied to the inside of the side rails.

1. Measure:

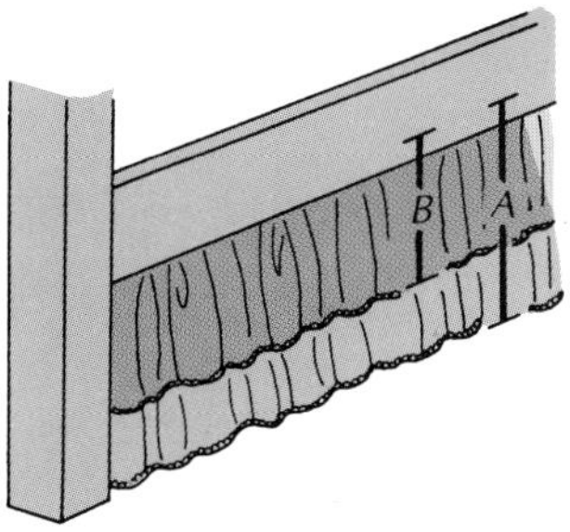

B
A
1½"
rail
floor

A = distance from 1½" above bottom of rail to floor
B = 4" less than A

Cut and piece two sets of strips for sides of bed and one set for ends, each 2½x finished length.

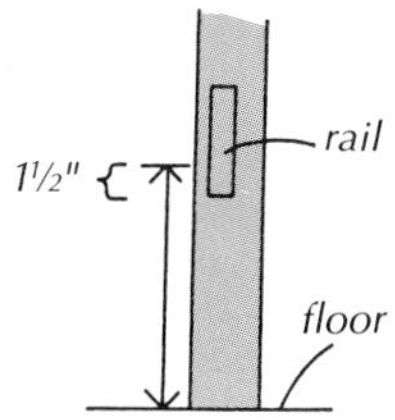

side
bed
side
end

2. Finish the sides and lower edges with a rolled edge.

3. For each ruffle, machine baste top edges of the two fabrics together. Pin Gosling Shirring tape on **wrong side**, even with top raw edge. **Machine baste** in place.

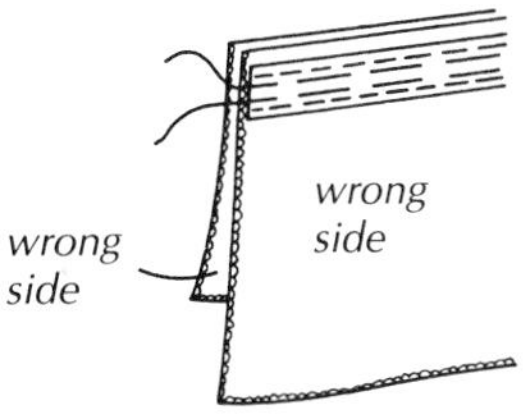

wrong side
wrong side

4. Pull cords to gather to fit each bed section. Permanently stitch just below bottom edge of tape to secure gathers. To save shirring tape for other projects, remove basting to remove shirring tape from ruffle.

5. Sew Velcro **hook** tape to **right side** of ruffle ½" from top edge.

6. Adhere strip of adhesive-backed Velcro **loop** tape along inside of each rail ½" up from bottom edge.

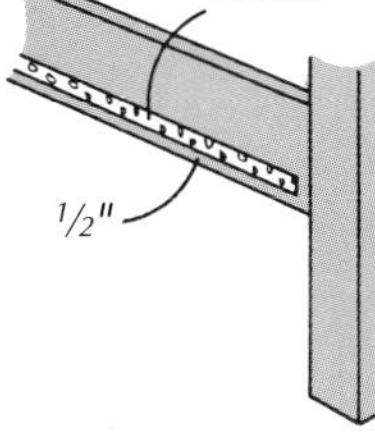

Velcro
½"

NOTE: You'll have lots of each type of Velcro left over. Save it for other similar projects, such as the sink skirts on pages 43 and 47.

7. Install ruffles on inside of footboard and side rails.

8. Quik Trak™ Upholstered Walls

Brad Hartley from Quik Trak introduced us to this wonderful wall-upholstering technique. With this easy-to-install track, quilt batting from Hobbs, and the striped fabric from Springs, the room went through a total transformation!

Using strips of adhesive-backed plastic track with "jaws" that grip the fabric, you will be creating a series of Quik Trak "stretcher" frames on the wall, into which you will snap the fabric:

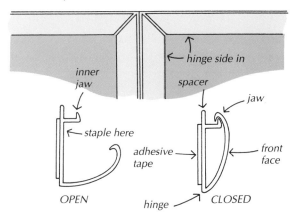

Also see the photo series on page 154.

You will need:

medium to lightweight fabric	Quik Trak
pruning shears or scissors	batting (if desired)
staple gun (electric is best)	measuring tape
staples	level

Use the full width of the fabric (if the design repeat allows). Make each "frame" 3" narrower than the usual fabric width. First, measure the width of the fabric, then plan the positioning of the "frames", keeping in mind pattern matching (page 150).

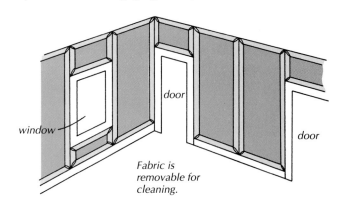

Fabric is removable for cleaning.

1. Mark Quik Trak positioning on the wall using a level and pencil.

2. Measure track to fit and cut from the hinge edge out to the jaws at a 45° angle to create the mitered corners. ("Eyeball" it, or use a 45° triangle or protractor.)

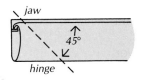

3. Open track, then peel off tape backing and lay the outer edge of track (the "jaw" side) carefully along your pencil lines. Press **firmly**. Staple to the wall every 1"-2", close to the inner jaw.

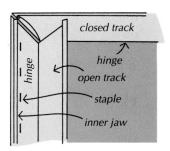

NOTE: Quik Trak is designed so that when one strip is mounted next to another, the edges just butt together when correctly installed.

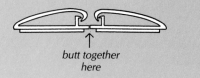

butt together here

4. Continue mounting track all around room. Don't worry about the small, oddly shaped areas around some woodwork; you will deal with them as you mount the fabric (see next page).

5. For padded walls, use 3/8"-thick batting for moderate fullness or 3/4"-thick batting (or two

layers) for a high-fashion, upholstered look. Cut batting slightly larger than each Quik Trak "frame." Staple to wall in a few places to hold in position. Holding scissors against Quik Trak hinge edge as guide, cut away excess batting. The fit does not have to be **exact**. Staple around edges every 6"-8" to secure.

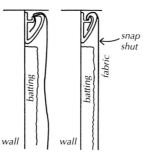

6. Cut fabric panels 3" longer than wall-mounted Quik Trak "frames."

7. Starting at a top corner, insert 1" of fabric into the Quik Trak channel, allowing 1" for the side edge. Continue tucking fabric into **top** channel, pressing track closed as you go. Fabric must hang straight, with edges parallel to Quik Trak.

8. Working from top to bottom, complete a side next, inserting fabric and locking track as you go. **Be sure** to keep the fabric straight. Complete the remaining side and then the bottom.

9. Check corners after all four sides have been completed. If necessary, open track slightly at corners and reinsert fabric neatly. Snap closed.

10. Continue for each panel.

Working on the Details

Working With Inside Corners

When mounting Quik Trak in a corner, leave enough space to mount fabric, using a piece of Quik Trak as a guide. If you forget to allow enough space between, you will **struggle** to get fabric snapped in place!

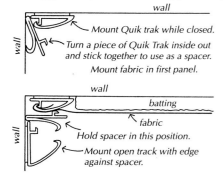

wall
— Mount Quik trak while closed.
— Turn a piece of Quik Trak inside out and stick together to use as a spacer.
Mount fabric in first panel.

wall
batting
fabric
Hold spacer in this position.
— Mount open track with edge against spacer.

Covering Gaps Between Panels

There will be a slight gap between fabric panels. To camouflage the gap, cut a 1/4"-wide piece of fabric the length of the panel and slide it into the channel with a screwdriver.

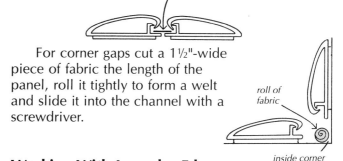

fabric strip

For corner gaps cut a 1½"-wide piece of fabric the length of the panel, roll it tightly to form a welt and slide it into the channel with a screwdriver.

roll of fabric

inside corner

Working With Irregular Edges

Sometimes window sills protrude beyond the casing width. Adhesive-backed, flexible foam weather stripping is the secret ingredient to handle these areas.

Cut weather stripping to fit around protruding sill. Remove backing and stick it snug to sill. Put double-faced tape on top.

Install fabric, leaving irregular side until last. Then work down from the top to the protrusion.

Carefully cut fabric to fit shape of sill, leaving ½" to tuck in later. Smooth fabric over weather stripping and continue to insert into the track below.

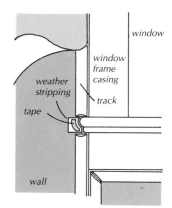

window
window frame casing
weather stripping
track
tape
wall

At protrusion, press to adhere fabric to tape, then use a table knife or screwdriver to gently push raw edge of fabric between weather stripping and window.

Wall Outlets and Switch Plates

These are easily handled, but first, **turn off** electrical power. Remove plates. Then install batting, trimming it away from outlet prior to snapping fabric into track. Once fabric is installed, feel for the electrical fixture, and make a small incision at the center. Then:

1. Cut an X to corners of electrical box as shown.

2. Fold flaps under so no fabric touches box.

3. Replace plate.

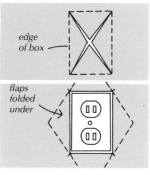

edge of box

flaps folded under

More information on Quik Trak installation and design ideas is available in their booklet (Resource List, page 155).

A Homey Bedroom

Linda's home in Portland's Sullivan's Gulch was built around the turn of the century, but in a very different style from Pati's Georgian Colonial. This "Portland style" home has nice architectural detailing, inside and out, but the impression is one of simplicity and comfort. We relied on a wonderful mix of fabric and color to bring this basic master bedroom alive.

We started with the bold cabbage rose print from P. Kaufmann. Moires, solids and calicos from Concord were chosen as complements. The pale, barely-peachy-pink walls make the room warm and cozy at night, without screaming **pink** (much to husband Bill's relief)! The tailored, striped Roman shade and the dark-colored "outlining" on the cornice, drape, quilt and pillow shams help balance the femininity of the floral fabrics, making a room inviting to all.

The quilt, though contemporary in design, fits right in with the homey look of the room. And the soft afghan, custom-designed and knit by knitting machine expert, Terri Burns, is the perfect finishing touch. Linda's 19-year-old cat, Wilma, obviously agrees!

1. FAST, EASY soft cornice serged with pearl cotton.
2. FAST, EASY side-drawn curtain and tieback serged with pearl cotton.
3. Roman shades.
4. Pillow shams.

1. Soft Cornice

To give substance to the lightweight fabric on these soft cornices, we sandwiched a layer of polyester fleece (page 154) between fabric and lining.

Mount Cornice Board and Measure

1. The cornice is attached to a wooden shelf mounted to the wall above the window, using angle irons.

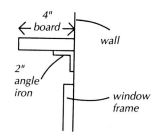

2. Cut fabric, lining and fleece 10" deep and wide enough to wrap around board, **plus** ½" to all sides for trimming as you serge.

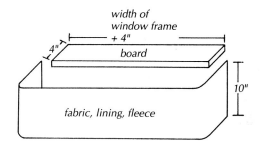

3. Cut strip of sew-on Velcro hook tape equal to length of cornice, **minus** 1½". Sew to **right side** of lining 1" from top.

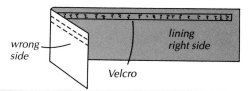

PRO TIP: To avoid waste when using both sew-on and self-adhesive Velcro, save other half of each kind for another window or other future project.

5. EASY round pillow from antique needlepoint.
6. Rocker cushion with ruffle.
7. EASY pleated dust ruffle made with Gosling Tape.
8. Pieced quilt with serged seams.
9. Machine knit afghan by Terri Burns.

4. Sandwich all layers, with fleece next to **wrong side** of fabric and lining. Pin.

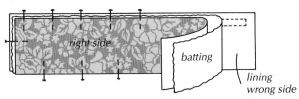

right side

batting

lining
wrong side

5. Serge edges with widest balanced stitch, using pearl cotton in upper and lower loopers. (Remember to **test first** every time you change thread **or** fabric.) Turn corners as described on page 144.

6. Cut a strip of adhesive-backed loop tape the same length as hook tape on cornice. Stick it in place on side and front edges of mounted cornice board. Mount cornice on cornice board.

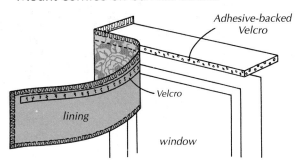

Adhesive-backed
Velcro

Velcro

lining

window

2. Side-Drawn Curtain

1. Measure desired width and length. Double the width, then add ½" seam allowances to sides. Add 3½" for casing at top and ½" for hem at bottom.

2. Cut fabric and lining, piecing as necessary. (Linda used Spartex's 90"-wide fabric for the lining so did not have to piece it.)

QUICK TIP: Generally, curtains look best when the fabric panels are each two to three times the window width. Linda didn't have enough fabric, so she used three lengths of fabric for two windows, splitting one in half and piecing.

half width | full width

3. With fabric and lining **wrong sides together** serge around all edges with the widest balanced stitch possible on your serger, using a heavy decorative thread in upper looper (or both loopers, for a reversible look). We used pearl cotton.

NOTE: To give bulk to the serged side and bottom edges (to match the edges on the padded cornice), we sandwiched strips of polyester fleece between fabric and lining along drape edges. Cut enough 1"-wide strips to equal one width and two lengths of each drape. (There is no need to piece them together.)

Insert fleece strip between fabric and lining along edge prior to serging with pearl cotton.

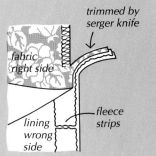

trimmed by
serger knife

fabric
right side

lining
wrong
side

fleece
strips

4. Mount curtain rod and hold fabric up to determine casing depth. Since you have already hemmed the drape with a rolled edge, adjust casing turn-under so drape hem just brushes floor. Mark top fold and casing stitching line.

5. Topstitch to create casing.

6. Hang drape and adjust fullness evenly.

To make tieback:

1. Using tape measure, pull curtain to one side. Mark spot on window frame where tieback should be attached. Note length of tieback.

2. Cut two strips of fabric and one strip of fleece for each tieback:

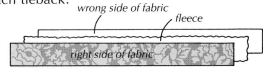

wrong side of fabric

fleece

right side of fabric

3. Sandwich fleece between **wrong sides** of fabric strips and serge all edges with a balanced stitch using pearl cotton in **both** loopers.

4. Sew plastic rings at each end of tieback and hook to cup hooks screwed into window frame.

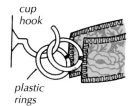

cup hook

plastic rings

3. Roman Shades

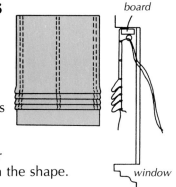

board

window

Roman shades are similar in construction to balloon shades, but have a crisper, more tailored look. A flat fabric panel is drawn up with cords threaded through rings. A wooden slat along or near the bottom helps maintain the shape.

You'll need the same basic hardware as listed for the balloon shades on page 23, plus fabric (crisp is best —it falls into the horizontal pleats better), lining, and a ¾"-wide wooden slat cut ½" shorter than the finished width of the shade.

1. Measure and cut fabric and lining.

*Width equals **inside** dimension of window frame plus seam allowances. (No wider, or shade will catch when it is raised and lowered!)*

Length equals height of window plus 1" overhang at top and seam allowance at bottom.

You'll need 3 lengths of Gosling Loop Shade Tape.

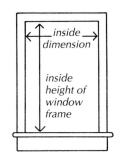

inside dimension

inside height of window frame

2. Stitch fabric to lining, **right sides together**, leaving an opening on **one** side for a 1"-wide slat casing located 5" above the bottom edge as shown.

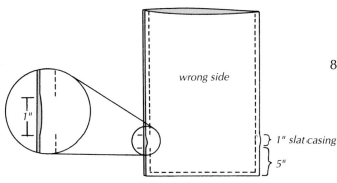

wrong side

1"

1" slat casing

5"

3. Trim seam allowances at bottom corners. Turn right side out and press.

right side

4. Stitch 1"-wide slat casing through both layers in line with side opening.

5. Place shade on table, lining side up. Carefully measure and mark tape positions with one strip down center and the other two ½" in from sides.

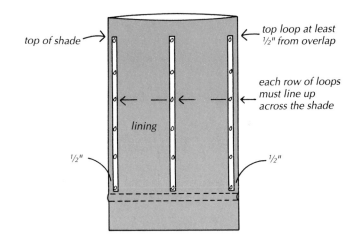

top of shade

top loop at least ½" from overlap

each row of loops must line up across the shade

lining

½"

½"

6. Carefully stitch tape in place through all layers, taking care that outer fabric does not pucker.

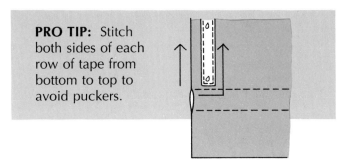

PRO TIP: Stitch both sides of each row of tape from bottom to top to avoid puckers.

7. String cords, tying securely to each bottom loop and leaving enough length to pull to one side and down to sill level.

8. Slide slat into casing.

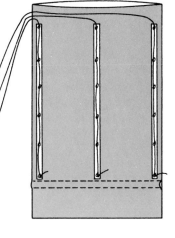

To mount shade:

1. Position mounting board in window and drill holes in board and window frame.

2. Place board along top of shade and position screw eyes in line with rows of Gosling tape.

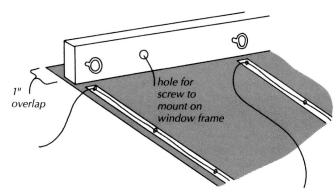

1" overlap

hole for screw to mount on window frame

3. Fold excess fabric over mounting board; staple in place, making sure it is **perfectly** even so blind will hang straight.

4. String cords through screw eyes.

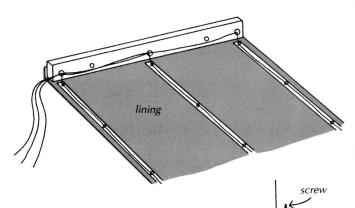

lining

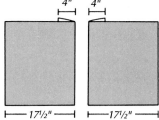

screw

blind cord

CROSS SECTION

5. Screw mounted shade to inside top of window frame. Mount cleat at side of window. (See page 21.)

6. With shade down, braid cords from top of window down approximately 12" (enough to comfortably grasp). Knot. Cut off extra cord.

7. Pull up shade and wrap cord around cleat. Smooth in folds and keep shade raised for a few days to "set" the folds.

4. Pillow Shams

These shams with their pieced border were made for queen-size pillows. Adjust the measurements for other pillow sizes.

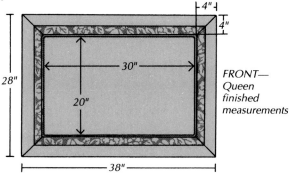

4"

4"

28"

30"

20"

FRONT— Queen finished measurements

38"

zipperless back opening

BACK

1. For front, cut 31"x 21" fabric rectangle.

2. Cut two backs, each 21½"x 21". Turn and press as shown.

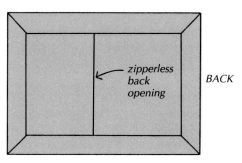

4"   4"

17½"   17½"

3. Overlap backs 4" and machine baste together.

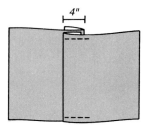

4"

4. Cut strips for border:

From solid fabric:
    4 strips—5"x 39
    4 strips—5"x 29
From print fabric:
    2 strips—2½"x 39
    2 strips—2½"x 29

5. **With right sides together**, stitch each print strip to its corresponding solid strip, as shown. Press print toward solid **over** seam as shown; machine baste raw edges together.

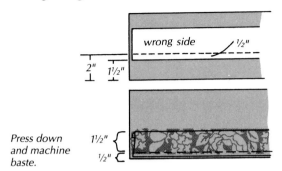

wrong side · ½"

2" · 1½"

Press down and machine baste. · 1½" · ½"

6. Create border rectangle from the four finished print/solid strips. Place strips right sides together and miter corners as shown. Trim seam allowances and press open.

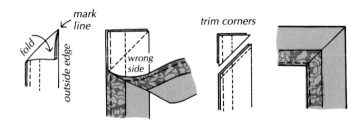

fold · mark line · outside edge · wrong side · trim corners

7. Make 3 yards of fabric (page 152) or serger piping (page 148) using a contrasting thread color.

8. Sew piping and border to sham fronts as follows:

Pin piping in place, clipping at corners. Machine baste.

front right side

machine baste

Pin border in place. Use zipper foot to stitch next to piping.

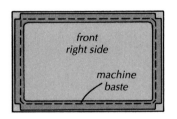

Trim seams and clip corners. Press border toward seams.

9. Sew border to sham back.

10. Stitch front to back, **right sides together**. Trim seams and clip corners. Turn and press.

11. Cut four batting strips of polyester fleece:

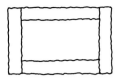

12. Tuck fleece between sham and border. Topstitch through all layers next to piping, using zipper foot. Stitch again in the well of seam between print and solid.

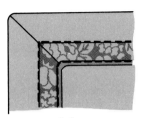

topstitch

13. Insert pillow.

5. Round Needlepoint Pillow

Choose a foam pillow form in a size compatible with your needlepoint. Make pillow backing out of complementary fabric.

1. For pillow backing, cut two half circles, adding seam allowance to centers for zipper, plus ½" seam allowance around outside. Insert zipper as shown. **Unzip zipper!!!**

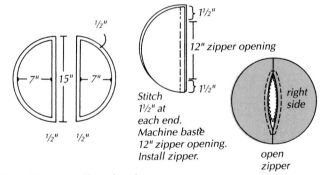

½" · 1½" · 12" zipper opening · 1½"

7" · 15" · 7"

½" · ½"

Stitch 1½" at each end. Machine baste 12" zipper opening. Install zipper.

right side · open zipper

2. Center pillow back over needlepoint design, **right sides together**; machine baste.

Trim away excess needlepoint.

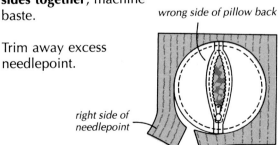

wrong side of pillow back

right side of needlepoint

3. Serge over stitching, using a 3/4- or 5-thread serger to securely finish edges.

4. Turn and press. Insert pillow form.

6. Rocker Seat Cushion

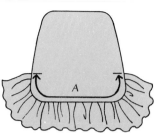

Linda's Boston rocker has been handed down through generations. And the old cushion has been around for at least 40 years! With its new cover, it will be good for many more. Like the previous one, the new cover has no zipper.

1. Cut front and back to size of existing cushion, **plus** seam allowances.

2. For ruffle, cut a 6"-wide fabric strip twice measurement A, above. Fold in half, lengthwise, **right sides together**; stitch short ends. Turn and press. Zigzag over cord placed next to seamline at remaining raw edges.

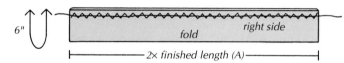

3. Pin ruffle to one cushion cover, **right sides together**, pulling on cord to draw up gathers to fit. Adjust gathers evenly. Stitch cushion covers, **right sides together**, leaving an 8" opening at back for turning.

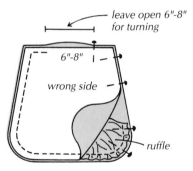

4. Insert pillow form and slipstitch opening closed.

7. Pleated Dust Ruffle

Gosling Folding Tape makes this project a breeze, "automatically" creating 3"-wide box pleats.

1. Valance strip height = desired drop + 1½" top seam allowance

   Length = 2½ x (A+A+B)

   Piece as needed.

2. Finish ruffle bottom with a rolled edge, barely skimming away the fabric edge with serger knife.

3. Machine baste Gosling Folding Tape along top edge. Tie cords together, then pull up to pleat. Press pleats in place.

4. Machine baste pleats in place along 1½" seamline. Remove Gosling tape (and save for another time!). Trim seam allowance to ½".

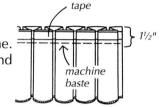

Complete as for dust ruffle in Eleanor's room (page 15).

8. Pieced Quilt

Linda had fun planning the design for and machine quilting this pieced bed covering. See page 25 to determine quilt dimension. This one for a queen size bed is 90" x 94".

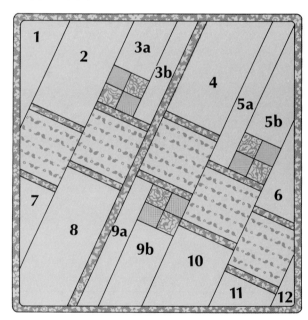

Make a scale drawing of your design, then transfer to a pattern made by taping newsprint together to full size. Number each odd shaped section as shown above on both scale drawing and full-size pattern. Then cut apart pattern along piecing lines. Cut fabric, adding seam allowances. Keep numbered pattern pieces pinned to each piece of fabric for identification.

Piece to create each long strip, then piece long strips together, using a 3/4 or 5 thread serger.

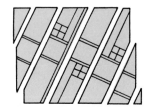

To machine quilt:

1. Working on a large, flat surface, make a "quilt sandwich" with polyester batting between the completed quilt top and backing fabric. (By using Spartex's 90"-wide fabric for quilt backing, we avoided piecing.) Use small, rust-proof safety pins to pin layers together, spacing pins no more than 6" apart (about the width of your hand) in both directions. Work from center out and make sure pins go through all layers.

2. Beginning at one corner, roll quilt firmly and tightly toward center, **parallel to piecing lines**. Hold in place with bicycle clips spaced evenly 6" to 10" apart.

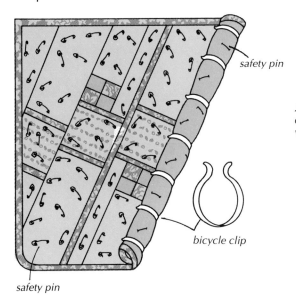

safety pin

safety pin

bicycle clip

> **NOTE:** If your piecing lines run parallel to sides of quilt, roll up from sides instead of corner.

3. Set up machine with clear nylon monofilament quilting thread on top and a thread color matching backing fabric in bobbin.

4. Beginning at center, with rolled half of quilt to your right (under sewing machine arm), stitch in the wells of the piecing seams. Remove pins as you reach them, only if in the way of stitching. Without removing bicycle clips, unroll quilt enough to stitch in well of next piecing seam. Continue until quilt is completely unrolled.

> **PRO TIP:** A walking foot or an even-feed attachment makes it easier to stitch smoothly and evenly through quilt layers. Check your machine manual or ask your dealer.

5. Repeat the rolling and stitching process, rolling from each of the remaining three directions. Remove all safety pins. Tie off thread tails on reverse side of quilt.

Binding the quilt:

To finish, bind outer edges of quilt with matching or contrasting bias binding.

1. Cut and piece a strip of fabric equal to the measurement of the perimeter of the quilt, plus 1", and three times the desired finished width, plus ½". Press under ½" along one long edge.

2. Pin binding along edge of quilt top, **right sides together**. Machine stitch through all layers. Miter corners as necessary (page 110).

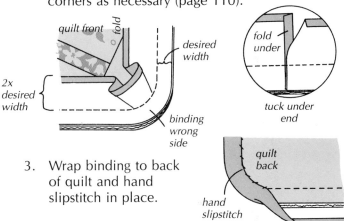

quilt front
fold
desired width
2x desired width
binding wrong side
fold under
tuck under end

3. Wrap binding to back of quilt and hand slipstitch in place.

quilt back

hand slipstitch

9. Afghan by Terri Burns

Terri Burns is a wonderfully creative designer and knitting machine expert. Her Trends Bulletin, **Knitting Machines**, is the perfect introduction to this fascinating handcraft. Write to Palmer/Pletsch to order bulletin and/or the free afghan pattern. (See page 159.)

Hand-painted Contemporary Bed & Bath

What do you do when you know exactly what you want for your next decorating project, but you can't find the "right" fabrics? World-renown textile designer Suzanne DeVall has the answer for you! Paint your own fabric using her fabulous fabric paints. Her work adorns hotels, yachts and the private domains of celebrities, including Carol Burnett and Donald Trump.

Suzanne developed her own line of 100% colorfast textile paints that actually meld with the fabric and do not stiffen when dry. Direct sunlight is not detrimental —a distinct advantage for home decorating fabrics that hang at windows! After the fabric is painted, it can be washed with a mild solution of soap such as Woolite or dish detergent. Or, the fabric can be dry cleaned.

Our instructions here just skim the surface of the possibilities. Many additional designs techniques can be used. Suzanne's kits include a how-to video, plus six paint colors and three foam brushes (1", 2" and 3" wide). See the Resource List on page 155 for ordering information.

The hand-painted, fabrics for Suzanne's contemporary bed and bath were created using 115"-wide fabric from Spartex. This extra-wide fabric virtually eliminates piecing, making the projects quicker, easier and less costly.

Before starting your first painting project, practice your designs on fabric scraps, referring to the product directions and the helpful hints.

Helpful Hints for Hand Painting Fabric

- Do not prewash fabric; the sizing in the fabric prevents paints from running. It's best to use fabrics with at least 40% cotton or other natural fiber, though we do love the look of it on Ultrasuede.

- The paints will bleed through the fabric, so protect the work surface with a 4'x 8' plywood panel or a non-porous material.

- These paints can be washed away with soap and water while wet, but **not** after they have dried.

- Suzanne's paints are premixed. Add white to lighten, black to darken, or water to dilute for a watercolor effect. Mix colors together to create new ones, too!

- Dampen brush with water first, then dip into paint. Do not saturate brush with paint. Paint will flow onto fabric and take on the appearance of a watercolor painting. If you use chintz (glazed surface), paints will not bleed as much and the resulting pattern will have crisper edges, not the softness of watercolors.

- It's easier to paint all of a single color at one time instead of completing each multi-colored design, then the next. You can cut designs from sponges and "stamp" design in place after dipping sponge forms into paint. Use a foam brush to fill in background or dab color on with a sponge.

- Try sponging another color over a previously painted section for added depth and dimension.

- Allow the paint to air dry. It is not necessary to heat-set the finished painting.

1. *Hand-painted duvet cover from Spartex 115" Doubleglaze fabric—NO PIECING!*
2. *Headboard using a hollowcore door, Quik Trak, Hobbs batting and hand-painted fabric.*
3. *Wall-mounted, hand-painted canopy tied back with mop cord from Hollywood Trims.*
4. *Tailored dust ruffle with inverted pleats.*
5. *EASY hand-painted pillows.*
6. *Hand-painted vanity table and re-covered bench.*
7. *Cube table skirted in fabric using Quik Trak.*

The painting over the bed is by Nobu Nakamuro. The little dog's name is Tu-Mika. And Suzanne even painted her shoes!

1. Duvet Cover

We painted the fabric, then made this duvet cover to fit an existing down comforter. We cut the front and back pieces from white Spartex fabric making them each 1" larger all around than the desired finished size.

Suzanne free-hand painted the floral design in the center of the duvet cover. If you're a little timid about the process, you may want to make a **light** pencil sketch of your design directly on the fabric first.

To paint the fabric:

1. Use push pins to secure central portion of fabric panel to work surface, making sure it is pulled taut.

2. The pattern repeat forms a grid. Using 1"-wide masking tape, mask the fabric as shown to create that grid. Use a T-square to make sure the outer edge is perfectly square.

3. Paint the chosen design, moving and rearranging fabric on work surface as needed.

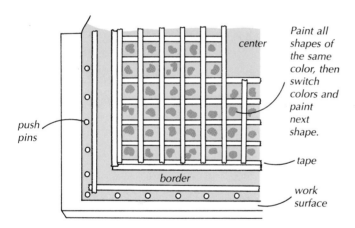

Paint all shapes of the same color, then switch colors and paint next shape.

center

push pins

border

tape

work surface

DESIGNER TIP:
To paint the design, we used the top edge of the foam brushes to create strokes like these:

4. After painting the entire piece and allowing to dry, remove the masking tape and paint in the solid area, using a sea sponge.

DESIGNER TIP: Don't be afraid to paint your own design. Suzanne says it's virtually impossible to make a mistake!

Construct the duvet cover as shown on page 58. When completed we wrapped and tied corners with natural mop cord braid from Hollywood Trims.

2. Headboard

We used an inexpensive hollow-core door from a lumber yard to create the padded headboard (the perfect size for a king sized bed). To make quick work of attaching the hand-painted fabric, we mounted Quik Trak (Resource List, page 157) on the door. First we painted a piece of white fabric the size of the headboard, plus 1" on all four sides.

1. To mount the headboard, screw the door to wall studs. Then apply Quik Trak, batting and hand-painted fabric. (See page 28 for how-to's.)

fabric

2. Finish top and side edges of door with braid stapled in place. Glue a strip of painted fabric over staples using fabric glue such as Sobo.

braid piping

PRO TIP: You may want to Scotchguard the headboard and trim to cut down on cleaning.

3. Canopy

Suzanne already had these wonderful architectural brackets, salvaged from an old house—which made a wonderful "frame" for our fabric canopy. First, we stapled Quik Trak to the pieces as shown.

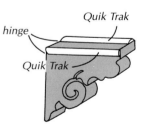

Quik Trak

hinge

Quik Trak

After mounting the pieces on the wall, we screwed a length of door molding to the front edges as a stabilizing framework on which to drape the sponge-painted fabric. (To sponge-paint, dip a sea sponge into paint and dab randomly over the fabric.)

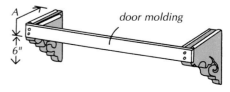

door molding

A

6"

We cut fabric for the canopy to match the distance between architectural pieces, **plus** 2". For the depth, we added 6" to measurement A (the **combined measurements** of the top edge of the architectural bracket and the width of the front board), then **doubled** the total.

Before snapping the canopy into the Quik Trak, we pressed under ½" on the short ends of the fabric, then folded it in half lengthwise, **wrong sides together**, and pressed a crease which became the front edge:

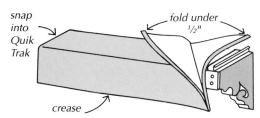

To paint the side drapes, we masked the fabric with tape to create "stripes" of sponged-on paint. Each panel was cut twice the desired finished width. The length equalled bracket to floor, plus hems. Panel sides and bottom were roll-edge finished.

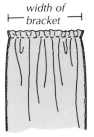
width of bracket

While snapping side panel into the track on inside of brackets, we hand gathered it to fit. If you prefer, machine easestitch the top edge, then draw up to fit.

We tied the side drapes back with natural braid from Hollywood Trims and made a tassel accent by rolling and glueing natural-colored mop cord, also from Hollywood Trims.

roll and glue

4. Dust Ruffle

We designed a simple dust ruffle for this project, using a coordinating solid-colored fabric. It was snapped into place on the box spring frame using Quik Trak.

1. For the ruffle, cut and piece fabric to equal two lengths and one width of the box spring, **plus** 60". Cut it twice the desired drop from top of box spring frame, **plus** 2".

drop

2. Fold ruffle in half lengthwise and press the fold for a "finished" bottom edge. Create a 6"-deep inverted pleat at ruffle center and pin in place. Pin-mark box spring width (corners of bed) at raw edge of ruffle.

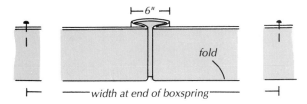
fold
width at end of boxspring

3. Form 6" deep inverted pleats at each pin-marked corner. Pin in place.

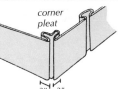
corner pleat
3" 3"

4. Locate center of each side of ruffle and create a 6"-wide inverted pleat at those locations. Pin. Stitch across top of all pleats.

5. Snap ruffle into Quik Trak stapled to box spring frame, starting at head of bed and working all the way around to the other side at the head of bed.

NOTE: Quik Trak will work only if you have a surface to staple into. Otherwide construct dust ruffle as shown on page 15.

5. Pillows

We used scraps of the hand-painted fabrics created for the bedroom to make a variety of interesting pillows to pile on the bed.

New pillow shams cover existing square European bed pillows. They were constructed as shown on page 54 (without ruffles) using painted fabric for the front and plain for the back. We added trim while seaming the pieces together, ending it just shy of each corner so we could wrap and tie "ears" to match the coverlet.

For textural and color contrast we added standard throw pillows with Ultrasuede covers featuring fat, contrasting piping caught in the seams.

We popped the bed pillows into pillowcases and tied the ends with heavy braid. Easy and effective!

6. Vanity and Bench

The vanity is a garage-sale find painted to match Suzanne's decor! We removed the bench seat by removing the screws and stapled Quik Trak to the seat bottom, 2" in from the outer edges. We snapped hand-painted fabric in place and replaced the seat. Suzanne also painted the legs to blend with the painted fabric seat cover.

7. Cube

An inexpensive laminated cube became our bedside table, softened with fabric snapped into place on Quik Trak. Since it's difficult to staple into plastic laminate, the adhesive backing alone holds the track along the top edge of the cube.

The Bathroom

Hand-painted drapes and valance soften the hard surfaces in this contemporary bath adjoining Suzanne's bedroom. Suzanne created a color scheme that blends with the existing wallpaper and with the bedroom (since there is no door separating the two rooms).

We mounted the flat valance on Quik Trak, stapled to the ceiling, following the angle at the front edge of the tub. The drapes are mounted on 18"-long pieces of Quik Trak mounted behind the valance track at each end. (The Quik Trak was mounted with hinged edge toward the windows.)

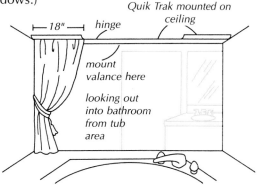

Quik Trak mounted on ceiling

18" hinge

mount valance here

looking out into bathroom from tub area

For the valance we cut a fabric panel 20"-wide and the length of the track, **plus** 1". After folding it in half lengthwise, **wrong sides together**, we snapped it into the Quik Trak, turning the short ends to the back to conceal the raw edges. The side drapes were created, mounted in the track and tied back with cord and tassel as shown for the bed drapes (page 41).

Roller Shades

We love Suzanne's roller shades in the bathroom windows! She painted fabric for the shade in a floral pattern, and painted the "non-sticky" side of fusible shade backing (page 155) in a stripe. When fused together, mounted and hung, the stripe on the backing shadows through to the front, creating a unique design. It also shows at the top of the finished shade when it's rolled up. (Mount the completed shade on the wooden roller as described on page 59.) We glued trim and tassels from Hollywood Trims at the bottom for design interest and to weight the shade so it hangs evenly.

1. EASY sink skirt with balanced stitch and rolled edges in pearl cotton; Gosling tape shirring.
2. Appliqued towels and washcloths with balanced stitch in pearl cotton on band edges.
3. EASY, FAST Gosling tape-smocked window valance with rolled-edge finish in pearl cotton.
4. Gosling tape-smocked wastebasket cover with rolled edges. Border trim finished in balanced stitch.
5. Toilet paper holder finished like wastebasket.
6. Quilted toilet seat and tank top covers.
7. Fabric-covered walls— using STARCH!

The Attic Bath

This little bath tucked away in the attic went from "Plain Jane" white to cheerfully floral with Waverly fabrics. We starched fabric to the walls and ceiling and added finishing touches with a shirred sink skirt and bathroom accessories. Hanging the framed print **below** the window (who ever heard of such a thing?) was the final flourish in our magical makeover.

1. Gathered Sink Skirt

This skirt dresses up a corner sink. We mounted it with Velcro glued to the underside of the sink. Sink skirts stay cleaner when mounted underneath the sink lip, rather than on top where they catch more drips and require more frequent laundering!

1. Measure from floor to up under sink rim at least 1". Cut fabric that length and 2½ times the finished width.

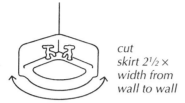
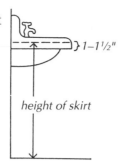

cut skirt 2½ × width from wall to wall

height of skirt

}1–1½"

2. Cut a strip from striped fabric for trim. Serge long edges with a balanced stitch using decorative thread.

QUICK TIP: Make enough trim for towels, wastepaper basket, and toilet paper holder at the same time.

3. Topstitch trim in place 8" above bottom edge.

4. Finish bottom and sides with rolled edges using decorative thread.

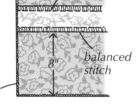

topstitch border

balanced stitch

rolled edge

8"

5. **On wrong side**, sew Gosling Smocking Tape (page 153) to top edge. Pull cords to smock to finished width. Tie off cords.

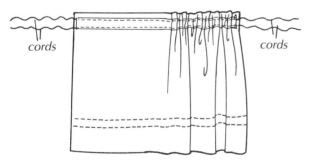

cords   cords

6. Sew a strip of Velcro over smocking along top edge on **right side** of skirt.

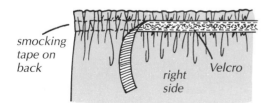

smocking tape on back

right side

Velcro

7. Using a hot glue gun, glue a strip of Velcro to underside of sink rim. Cool until firm.

8. Position skirt under rim of sink, pressing Velcro strips together.

2. Appliqued & Embellished Towels

These were quick and easy to make—with dramatic results! We repeated the sink skirt trim treatment and added rose appliques cut from the all over print and applied with transfer web (page 155).

1. Place rough side of a transfer web on **wrong side** of printed fabric. Press 3 seconds with a hot, dry iron. Let cool.

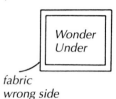

Wonder Under

fabric wrong side

2. Cut desired shape from fabric using a **sharp** scissors.

3. Carefully peel off paper backing.

cut shape with sharp scissors

4. Position on towel. Cover with damp press cloth. Fuse 10 seconds with iron on wool steam setting.

3. Window Valance

This window was a decorator's challenge. We didn't want to cover the window, but we did want a fabric treatment to soften it. Since the windows swing open from side hinges, a traditionally mounted valance would get in the way. So we used hinged curtain rods that meet in the middle, covering them with valances smocked with Gosling tape.

1. Cut each valance 2½ times the window width and twice the desired finished length, plus 1".

2. Turn under short edges ¼" and stitch or finish with serging, trimming away ¼" as you stitch.

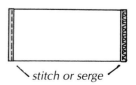

stitch or serge

3. Fold and press long edges of valance to inside, overlapping 1" in center as shown. Finish top and bottom folds with rolled edges using a contrasting decorative thread in upper looper.

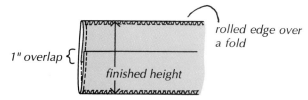

1" overlap {

finished height

rolled edge over a fold

4. Center Gosling tape on wrong wide of valance and stitch in place. Stitch 1¼" from top edge to form casing for curtain rod.

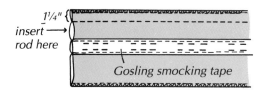

1¼"
insert → rod here

Gosling smocking tape

5. Pull cords to smock to fit rods. Tie to secure. Slide casing over rod. Tug on valance to even out folds.

4. & 5. Smocked Wastebasket Cover and Toilet Paper Holder

We made both of these accessories following the same basic steps shown for the valance (eliminating the top casing).

The finished wastebasket cover is ¾" taller than the basket with Gosling tape at top and bottom edges. Stitch on the tape. Seam the two short ends together, then draw up cords for a snug fit over basket. Slipstitch a strip of trim (matching sink skirt trim) to finished cover.

Make the paper holder with a single strip of Gosling tape down the center. Seam the ends and draw up cords to fit.

6. Quilted Toilet Seat and Tank Top Covers

We followed the subtle diamond pattern to quilt the print in these covers. Look for a "built-in" quilting design or chalk mark a pattern onto the covers.

1. Make paper patterns by tracing shape of seat and tank top. Cut batting to match seat and tank. Cut fabric and lining for each, adding 4" all around for casings.

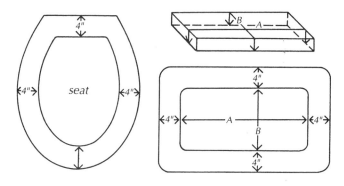

seat

4"

B — A

4"

A

B

2. Sandwich batting between fabric and lining. Machine quilt through all layers. Serge-finish outer edges.

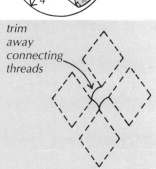

batting
wrong side lining
4"

QUICK TIP: To move easily from one quilting diamond to the next, raise presser foot, and slide to next position. Backstitch at beginning and end of each diamond. Clip threads.

trim away connecting threads

For seat cover:

1. Press under 1" around outside edge. Tuck cord into fold and stitch ¾" from edge, leaving 2" back opening.

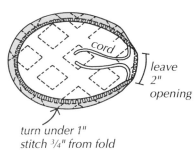

cord
leave 2" opening
turn under 1"
stitch ¾" from fold

2. Place on seat and pull cord to draw fabric snugly around seat. Tie securely.

For tank cover:

1. Miter corners.

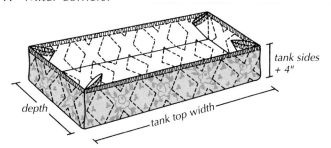

tank sides + 4"

depth

tank top width

2. Trim away excess fabric in corner miters.

3. Create casing as shown for seat cover and fit completed tank cover over tank top.

7. Starched Fabric Wall Covering

We used starch to adhere fabric to the walls and ceiling—a technique developed by Judy Lindahl. It works on any smooth, non-absorbent wall surface. Choose a tightly woven fabric for best results. Fabric **can** be removed and starch washed from wall.

You will need liquid starch, a large sponge, bucket, pushpins, plumb bob, metal-edged ruler and plenty of single-edge razor blades. Protect the floor with painter's drop cloths.

1. Cut fabric to desired lengths, plus 3" (and an allowance for pattern repeats—see page 150). When figuring the number of lengths needed, allow for 1" overlap from panel to panel. Press out any distinct creases.

> **PRO TIP:** We recommend testing a piece on the wall to determine the amount of shrinkage and to try out the technique. Let test sample dry thoroughly.

2. Determine starting place. (Try to avoid starting a panel at a corner.)

3. Establish a plumb line (perfectly perpendicular to floor), using chalk-covered plumb bob or string.

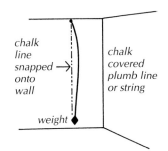

chalk line snapped → onto wall

chalk covered plumb line or string

weight

4. Pour starch into bucket and apply liberally to wall, using a large sponge and starting at ceiling. Place

fabric on starched wall with 1" extending above ceiling line. Pushpin in place. Smooth fabric in place with sponge dipped in starch. Continue applying starch to wall, then to fabric as you smooth it in place. Extra fabric at top and bottom will be trimmed after drying.

5. Repeat for each panel, overlapping panels slightly and matching print from panel to panel as required.

6 Let dry completely.

7. Trim top and bottom edges, using metal-edged ruler and **sharp** blade. Once starched and dried, fabric cuts like paper.

8. For neat seaming between panels, position ruler in center of overlapped seams. Cut with sharp blade from top to bottom in one continuous stroke through both layers.

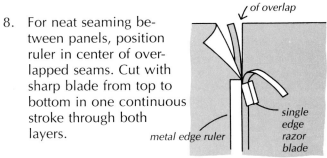

trim down center of overlap

metal edge ruler

single edge razor blade

9. Remove loose trimmings and apply starch with sponge to press cut edges together again.

> **PRO TIP:** Starching fabric to the ceiling is a real **challenge**—it just doesn't want to stay put! Enlist a friend's help and use lots of pushpins! If you can find it, concentrated liquid starch holds better. If fabric doesn't adhere perfectly, apply another light coat of starch!

10. Add border stripe last. Cut stripes carefully. For fast, easy and accurate cutting, use a rotary cutter and mat. You may want to decoratively serge cut edges before applying to the wall. See page 118.

For more detailed information about starching fabric to walls, see **Decorating with Fabric** by Judy Lindahl (see Product List, page 159).

We also starched fabric onto an old mirror frame—a quick and easy transformation.

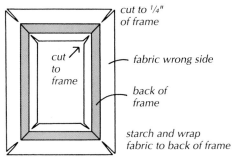

cut to 1/4" of frame

cut to frame

fabric wrong side

back of frame

starch and wrap fabric to back of frame

Cleo's Bath

Our friend Cleo's unique living room and dining room are featured on pages 78-82. This adjoining bath paled by comparison. There was nothing to do but continue our floral/stripe story with Concord fabrics to create a softly feminine bath with decorator towels, a fabric shade and cloud valance, sink skirt and shower curtain and a pretty mirror treatment.

1. Sink skirt with rolled-edge hem.
2. Shower curtain shirred with Gosling Tape.
3. SIMPLE pouf valance.
4. Window shade with decorative balanced stitch.
5. Fabric-covered mirror frame.
6. Appliqued towels with rolled edges.
7. EASY Round tablecloth with rolled edge.

1. Sink Skirt

Most wall-hung sinks aren't very attractive. This one got the treatment with a ruffled sink skirt. We attached it under the lip of the sink and created a separate ruffled apron that hides the wide edge of the sink. Thanks to Velcro hook and loop tape it can be removed easily for laundering.

PRO TIP: We bought one length of self-adhesive Velcro and one length of sew-on Velcro. We used the self-adhesive Velcro on the sink edge and under the lip and stitched sew-on Velcro to the underside of the skirt and ruffled apron.

We made the skirt 2½ times the distance around the sink and used Gosling Shirring Tape with three cords to draw it up to fit. See page 153. The bottom edge is finished with a decorative rolled edge.

For the ruffled apron:

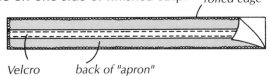

1. Determine desired finished depth and cut two strips of fabric that width plus ½" and long enough to fit around sink plus ½". With wrong sides together, roll-edge finish. Center and stitch Velcro tape on one side of finished strip.

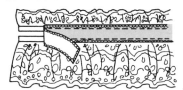

rolled edge

Velcro   *back of "apron"*

2. Cut second strip of fabric 1½"-wide and long enough to fit around sink, plus ½". Finish with rolled edges all around. Lap finished edges over pre-gathered lace trim and stitch.

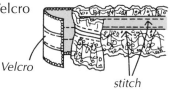

3. Center and stitch completed ruffle over Velcro stitching.

Velcro

stitch

2. Shower Curtain

We used the same 3-cord Gosling Shirring Tape as on the sink skirt to shirr the shower curtain to fit the tub opening. The double ruffle is a single

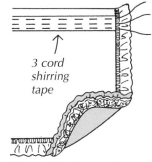

3 cord shirring tape

layer of fabric with a rolled edge and a layer of narrower lace, gathered to fit one side and the bottom edge of the shower curtain. We serged it to the curtain and pressed the seam toward the curtain.

Because Cleo had a set of decorative shower curtain rings, we made buttonholes at the top edge of the **finished** curtain, spacing them to match the eyelets in the plastic shower curtain liner that hangs behind it. Be careful not to stitch buttonholes over shirring cords. (The shirring tape does have loops to catch into inexpensive wire shower curtain rings if that's what you prefer.)

The braided tieback combines strips of all the fabrics with plastic drapery rings at both ends to catch on a cup hook screwed to the wall.

3. Pouf Valance

It just takes two curtain rods and a simply sewn valance with top and bottom rod pockets to make this elegant and easy valance.

1. To determine desired finished valance length, mount top rod and drop a tape measure from rod as shown. Cut valance that length plus enough additional length for two pockets to fit the curtain rods of your choice. Cut it 2½ times the window width.

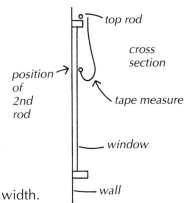

top rod

cross section

position of 2nd rod

tape measure

window

wall

2. Finish valance ends with rolled edges or narrow machine-stitched hems. Press under and stitch rod pockets.

3. Mount bottom rod at desired location. Insert curtain rods into rod pockets. Adjust poufs.

PRO TIP: For extra pouf, starch the fabric. You can also tuck loosely wadded tissue paper into the bottom of the valance to help form the poufs (but not in a steamy bathroom!).

4. Window Shade

Custom-made, fabric window shades are easy to make using a fusible backing to add the necessary body. See Resource List, page 155, for brand names. We finished the edges with a balanced three-thread stitch, although it's not necessary to finish fabric shade edges. We used a contrasting thread for emphasis. We removed the original shade from the roller and replaced it with the new one so we didn't have to remove and replace shade brackets.

Consider adding fabric appliques to your shades using transfer web in the same manner described for the decorator towels, below.

5. Mirror Frame

The existing mirror in this bath was frameless. What a difference a simple fabric-covered frame made! It rests on top of the mirror, covering at least ¼" of the mirror all around.

1. After determining desired frame width, cut frame sections from foam-center board such as Foamcore and join with duct tape. Glue a layer or two of batting to front of finished "frame."

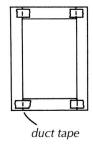

duct tape

2. Cut a rectangle of fabric 1½" larger all around than outer dimensions of "frame."

3. Make contrasting welting using fat cord for filler and allowing for a 1½" seam allowance. Stitch to fabric rectangle, clipping seam allowance at corners and overlapping at one short end.

welting

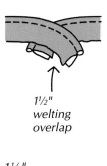

fabric right side

1½" welting overlap

1½"

4. Position and wrap fabric over frame with welting at outer edges. Tape to back of frame with duct tape or use fabric glue.

5. Cut out center of fabric, leaving a 1½" allowance and clipping to corners as shown. Wrap fabric to back side and tape in place. If desired, glue or tape welting on inner edge of frame.

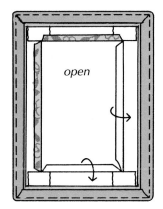

open

frame

6. Mount completed frame on wall over outer edge of mirror using fine nails and double-faced sticky craft tape. Carve out a hole in the foam-board frame wherever it rests over mirror clips so frame rests directly against mirror all around.

6. Decorator Towels

Special towels are fun to make to complete any bathroom. Scout the linen department in your favorite store for ideas. (Also see the towels in Barbara Weiland's guest room/office makeover on page 124, Eleanor's Bath, page 21, and The Upstairs Bath, page 44). Striped fabric bands finished with decorative rolled edges were machine stitched in place with ruffled eyelet trim tucked between the layers at both edges.

towel

It was easy to fuse intricately cut sections of the floral print to the completed towels using transfer web. (See page 155.) First fuse a piece of the web to the wrong side of the area including and surrounding the motif you plan to use. Leave the backing paper on while you cut out the design, then remove, position the applique and fuse.

Each towel is slightly different because we used different sections of the design for the appliques. It was fun to experiment!

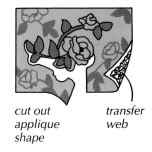

cut out applique shape

transfer web

7. The Tablecloth

Again we've used our favorite round, to-the-floor cloth, finished with a simple rolled edge. See page 13.

Kelsey's Daisy Kingdom Room

Kelsey's room is a wonderful retreat for any young girl, done up in romantic prints from Daisy Kingdom. As your child grows, you can simply replace toy bins with girlish books, photos and mementos. We recommend pretreating fabrics for a child's room with a stain-repellant finish such as Scotchguard before assembling the components.

1. Padded Waterbed Frame

Kelsey's bed is an "economy model" waterbed. Since waterbed frames are hard and uncomfortable, we padded the frame with foam and covered it with Concord's coordinating chintz.

1. *Padded waterbed frame—NO SEW!*
2. *Padded headboard with serger braid (rolled edge over cord with Ribbon Floss).*
3. *Comforter with decorative, balanced stitch serging—Ribbon Floss.*
4. *Pillows with serger piping—Ribbon Floss over cord on Seams Great.*
5. *Shirred top molding—EASY SEW!*
6. *Window cornice—rolled edge over heavy cord with Ribbon Floss.*
7. *Warm Window shades.*
8. *Fabric picture frames with Ribbon Floss rolled edges.*

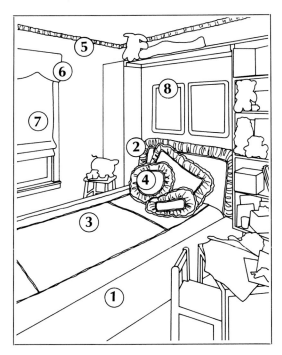

NOTE: A medium- to heavyweight fabric is best. A lightweight fabric may need lining. Press fabric to remove wrinkles.

1. Cut 1½"-thick foam into pieces to fit foot- and sideboards, adding 3" to the height of each piece to wrap over and to inside of frame.

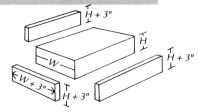

2. Using a hot glue gun and heavy-duty glue, attach foam to side- and footboards with bottom edges of foam even with bottom edges of frame and 3" extending above frame. Foam should meet at corners of frame.

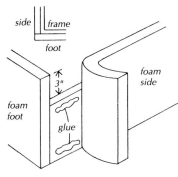

NOTE: Hot glue cools quickly so glue a little at a time and move quickly! Glue is **extremely hot**, so don't touch the glue or the gun tip. Do this work while "little fingers" aren't around.

3. Wrap and glue remaining foam to inside of frame.

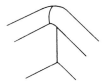

4. Measure padded frame and cut two sideboard and one footboard fabric panel, adding seam allowances at corners, plus 2", to sideboard panels to wrap to back of frame. Make each piece 5" wider than frame height.

5. Serge panels together using 4- or 5-thread stitch. Press to one side. Serge long edges to control raveling.

6. Beginning at the center of footboard, staple **right side** of fabric to inside of frame with ½"-wide cardboard upholstery strip on top of fabric and all edges 1½" below top edge of frame. (You'll wish you had four hands for this step!) Keep fabric on grain and space ¼"-long, heavy-duty staples every 4". Stop within 2" of inside corners.

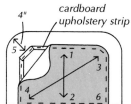

NOTE: If staples do not penetrate wood completely, tap with hammer until flat.

7. To make sure you allow enough fabric to go around corners, pull fabric to outside of frame and smooth over foam, adjusting so seam is lined up with corner. Pleat out excess fabric inside frame to form a neat corner. Pin.

8. Turn fabric back to inside of frame to finish stapling into corners and along side rail.

9. Continue stapling around corner and along sides, working the pinned-out excess fabric into corner.

outside corner

10. Beginning at center of footboard, pull fabric taut over foam, wrapping extra to underside. Staple. Wrap and staple extra sideboard fabric over ends at head of bed.

underside of bed frame

2. Padded and Covered Headboard

foam extends 1" beyond

plywood and headboard width

1. Make a paper template for desired size and shape of headboard. Kelsey's is 24" high and the width of padded bed frame. Cut headboard from ¾" plywood.

2. Glue 2"-thick foam to headboard allowing 1" extra on sides and top to wrap and staple to back.

3. To create "border" for shirring, position and staple cardboard strips 4" (or more) in from outer edge.

4. Staple an oversized piece of fabric to cardboard over inner section, pulling fabric taut and keeping it on grain. Place the first staples in numbered order on illustration. Trim away excess fabric next to outer edge of cardboard.

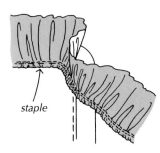

cardboard upholstery strip

5. Cut fabric strip for shirring 3 times the length of the outside edge and 6" wider than the border. Gather to fit around headboard at inner edge of border. Staple to cardboard, keeping gathers even. At inner top curves, draw up gathers a little tighter for even gathers at outside curve. Staple shirring to back of headboard.

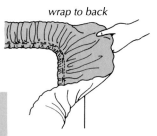

staple

wrap to back

DESIGNER TIP: Pad border with polyester batting to pouf and shape curve before stapling.

6. Cover staples with purchased braid or make your own and glue in place. We made ours with ribbon floss in the upper looper and did a rolled-edge over cord on both edges of a fabric strip.

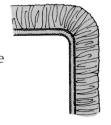

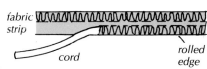

fabric strip

cord

rolled edge

3. Comforter

Kelsey's comforter is made from one of Daisy Kingdom's newest, pre-quilted designs, combining a central motif with side, top and bottom panels to achieve the required size.

NOTE: To determine finished comforter size, measure inside of bed frame and add 4" all around for tuck-in.

1. With **wrong sides together**, machine stitch top and bottom panel to center panel with a ¼"-wide seam allowance. Be careful to catch all layers in stitching. Use a roller or walking foot for even feeding. Then zigzag seam close to raw edges. This seemingly extra step is a sanity-saver for the next step!

right side

2. Serge over seam, using a 3-thread balanced stitch with ribbon floss in upper looper.

3. Finger press seam so decorative serging lays flat on comforter. Machine stitch at edge of serged seam to give appearance of decorative flatlocking. This is a sturdier seam finish for items that get heavy use.

NOTE: Decide which way you want the seam to lay so upper looper stitching will be consistent. For example, we decided to press the completed serging toward the center on Kelsey's comforter.

4. Complete comforter top, adding the two side panels.

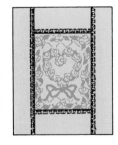

PRO TIP: Help serger over hump with a gentle tug when crossing seams to avoid thread build-up. Fold serger tails under before crossing seams; **do not cut them off** or serging will unravel.

5. Cut comforter backing from coordinating chintz to match finished size of comforter top. Bind outer edges of comforter to eliminate excessive wear from rubbing on inside of frame. To keep layers from shifting, bartack in each corner of center panel.

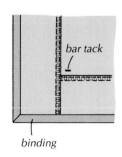

bar tack

binding

4. Pillows

The Daisy Kingdom line includes a pillow panel. We used the large panel for the pillow sham and made throw pillows from the other two. Use the same technique for the small pillows as shown for the sham.

Double-Ruffled Pillow Sham with Serger Piping

1. Cut flat lace and fabric ruffle twice the outside measurement of sham top, piecing ruffle strip as needed. Make fabric ruffle ½" wider than lace.

2. Make serger rolled-edge piping (page 148) with ribbon floss in upper looper. Machine stitch piping to sham front using zipper foot.

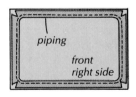

piping

front right side

3. Roll-edge finish one long edge of ruffle. Join short ends of ruffle and then lace with serged seams. **With wrong side of lace against right side of ruffle,** easestitch 5/8" and 3/8" from edge.

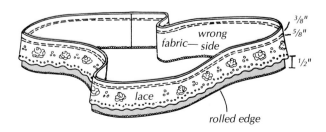

3/8"
5/8"
fabric— wrong side
1/2"
lace
rolled edge

4. **Right sides together**, pin ruffle to pillow with raw edges even; draw up easestitching to fit.

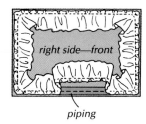

right side—front

piping

5. For back of sham, cut fabric same width as front and 6" longer than front. Cut in half at crosswise fold. Serge cut edges.

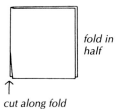

├── sham front ──┤
length   +6"

fold in half

↑
cut along fold

6. Press under 1" and stitch in place.

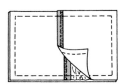

press under 1"

7. Pin backs to front, **right sides together**, with hemmed edges overlapping at center back for opening. Stitch, turn and press. Pop in the pillow!

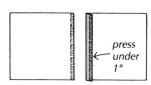

4. Shirred Top Molding

Cosmetic reasons inspired this shirred molding treatment—it hides poorly finished ceiling/wall joints in sheet rock. You might want to do it just because it's pretty!

1. For molding, cut 1"x 2" common lumber to fit measurement of two parallel walls. Cut lumber to fit remaining walls, less ¾" at each end.

PRO TIP: If using more than 1 board on a wall, butt sections together inside the shirring.

2. For each board, cut and piece a 5½"-wide strip of fabric **three times** the board length. Serge pieces together in ¼"-wide seams. Press seams to one side.

---

3. With **right sides together**, serge long edges of each strip to create a **long** tube. To turn tubes right side out, slip a ¼" dowel with a nail in one end inside the tube, tie the serger chain to the nail, then work the dowel through the tube and out the other end.

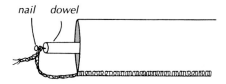

nail   dowel

4. Slide tubes over boards with seam centered on back of board.

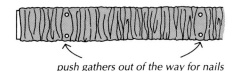

5. With someone to help, nail the covered boards in place at the wall/ceiling joint. Hide nails in the gathers, spacing them about every 18". Mount the longest pieces first. **Do not nail through gathers**.

push gathers out of the way for nails

6. Window Cornice

We used Daisy Kingdom's dust ruffle fabric to cover the window cornice in Kelsey's room. We followed the curve of the print rather than cutting it straight across the bottom as the fabric was printed.

1. Cut fabric, lining and thin quilt batting or polyester fleece the width of window plus 4" at each end, centering the curve or design in the window. Keep curves large and flowing rather than small and tight so you can serge around them easily. Set batting aside.

2. Serge bottom edge of fabric to lining, **wrong sides together**, using a wide rolled edge over heavy cording with ribbon floss in upper looper.

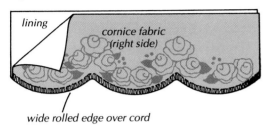

lining

cornice fabric (right side)

wide rolled edge over cord

3. Cut a 1"x 4" mounting board the width of window **plus** molding. Temporarily tack cornice to mounting board, centering the motif. Cut away excess fabric at sides, allowing ½" at each end for rolled-edge finish. Remove from board.

4. Roll-edge finish cornice ends. Slip batting or fleece between fabric and lining. Trim away excess batting as needed for **smooth** fit inside cornice.

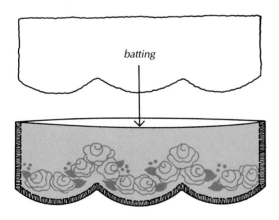

batting

5. Staple cornice to top of mounting board through all layers. Attach angle irons to bottom of mounting board and mount on window frame.

The
7. Warm Window®
INSULATED ROMAN SHADE SYSTEM

We used Daisy Kingdom panels, originally designed for draped windows, to create window shades for Kelsey's retreat, using Warm Windows (see Resource List, page 155) for the lining. Warm Windows improves the R factor (insulating factor) of window treatments. For example, double-pane windows have an R factor of R-1.8, but a single-pane window with the Warm Window system has an R factor of R-7.69! Insulation reduces heat loss in cold regions and keeps out unwanted solar heat radiation where it is hot.

The Warm Window system incorporates magnetic seals to achieve the maximum R value. The manufacturer recommends the seals in colder climates, however, we chose to eliminate them in our milder climate. Complete directions are available with the product.

1. For inside shade mount, cut fabric to fit inside window dimensions, **plus** 3" extra width and 12" extra length. (For outside shade mount, see Melissa's playroom, page 66.)

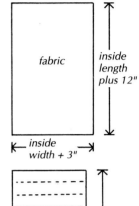

fabric

inside length plus 12"

inside width + 3"

2. Cut Warm Window the desired **finished** width and the desired finished length, **plus** 4" for mounting.

inside length plus 4"

inside width

> **NOTE:** For shades longer than 43" and shorter than 56", use 60"-wide Warm Window fabric. For finished shades longer than 56", piece Warm Window following instruction booklet available where you purchase Warm Window.

3. Place right side of fabric against smooth exterior lining side of Warm Window with top and side edges matching. Fabric will not lay flat due to the 3" extra width. Machine stitch ½" side seams. Serge through all layers **without cutting away any seam allowance.**

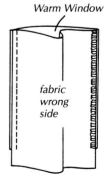

Warm Window

fabric wrong side

4. Turn right side out and smooth layers, allowing extra fabric width to wrap evenly to wrong side of shade.

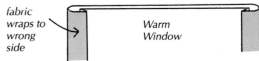

fabric wraps to wrong side

Warm Window

5. Press up a double 4"-wide hem at bottom of shade, placing fold at last Warm Window quilting line. Hand hem or machine edgestitch close to fold.

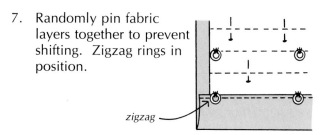

6. With shade **wrong side up** on flat surface, mark ring locations on every other quilting line, evenly spaced 8" to 12" apart across shade width. Rings at outside edges should be no more than 1¼" from edge.

4" double hem

4"

7. Randomly pin fabric layers together to prevent shifting. Zigzag rings in position.

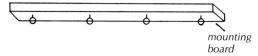

zigzag

8. Attach screw eyes or pulleys to 1"x 2" mounting board in line with rows of rings on shade.

mounting board

9. Staple shade to mounting board.

shade front

mounting board

10. Tie cord to each bottom ring in a square knot and apply Sobo glue to ends to prevent slippage. Thread cords through rings and screw eyes. Knot together. Screw mounting board in place inside window frame.

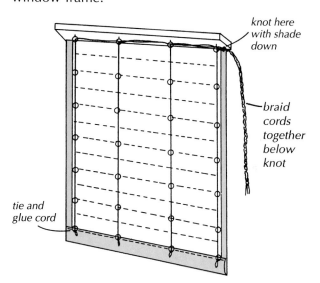

knot here with shade down

braid cords together below knot

tie and glue cord

8. Picture Frames

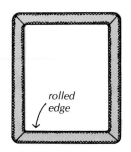

rolled edge

Rather than spend money for matting and framing a very inexpensive poster, we decided to serge our own "mat" and "frame".

1. For "mat," cut 2½"-wide strips of solid-colored fabric the measurement of each side of poster image area, **plus** 2". For "frame," cut similar strips, making them 2¼ wide.

2. Roll-edge finish one long edge of each strip.

3. Lay solid-colored strips on poster with rolled edges to inside over edge of print; pin, then stitch mitered corners to fit (page 35). Repeat with printed strips for "frame." When completed, "frame" should allow ¼" of "mat" to show.

4. Lay "frame" on top of "mat" and topstitch stitch together next to rolled edge of "frame." Roll-edge finish outer raw edges together, curving corners.

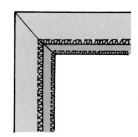

5. Now, check the size of your backing. Lay poster on top of original cardboard backing. Lay mat and frame, centered, over poster. If cardboard size does not match size of framed poster, cut a new cardboard backing to fit.

6. Glue poster to cardboard backing using spray-on craft glue. Then glue mat and frame, centered, over poster.

glue poster to cardboard backing

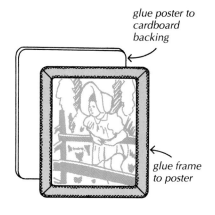

glue frame to poster

The Boys' Room

Not necessarily for boys only, this group of coordinating circus prints from Fabric Traditions inspired lots of creative ideas for transforming a basic bedroom from boring to fun. Bright primary colors make it a cheery spot for daytime play.

Keep durability in mind when choosing fabric, thread and serging techniques for a child's room. Pearl cotton is an excellent thread choice for items that get lots of wear because it's durable and washable. Be sure to tie off all serger tails and apply Fray Check seam sealant for added durability. See page 143.

1. *Duvet covers with pearl cotton balanced stitch.*
2. *Valance and roller shade with Decor 6 rayon balanced stitch and EASY appliques.*
3. *Basketball hoop hamper.*
4. *INSTANT starched wall decals.*
5. *Circus tent! (See page 60).*

1. Duvet Covers

A duvet cover (a large "pillowcase" for an existing comforter) makes quick-change bedroom redecorating easy and low-cost **and** keeps the comforter clean. These bunk bed duvets were made by surrounding a large design panel in the center with side, top and bottom panels in a coordinating stripe. The cover was made to match the size of the comforter.

For easy maintenance, consider making the back cover from sheeting fabric to eliminate the need for a top sheet. It makes for easy bedmaking—any child can do it. On laundry day, simply unzip and remove the comforter.

1. Cut and straight stitch top and bottom panels to central panel, **wrong sides together**, using ¼"-wide seams. Decoratively serge seams with wide, balanced 3-thread stitch, using pearl cotton in upper looper. **Do not** cut away serger tails. Finger press seam to one side so decorative serging shows. Topstitch close to outer edge of serging through all layers.

stitch first then decoratively serge

finger press up and topstitch

leave serger tails

2. Add side panels, following same steps.

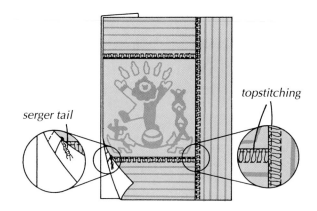

serger tail

topstitching

PRO TIP: Be prepared to help serger over hump when crossing serged seams to avoid thread build-up. Fold serger tails under before crossing seams; **do not cut them off** or serging will unravel.

3. Cut duvet back from a coordinating fabric, making same size as completed front. **Right sides together**, stitch front to back at bottom end, basting the zipper opening closed. Insert zipper using a centered application. **Unzip zipper.**

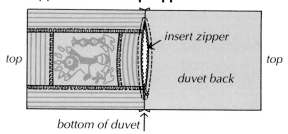

top

insert zipper

top

duvet back

bottom of duvet

4. Serge remaining edges using a 3/4- or 5-thread stitch for durability. Turn cover right side out and insert the comforter!

duvet back— wrong side

unzip first!

2. Valance and Roller Shades

For an easy window treatment, we made serged and shirred valances to slip over 4½"-wide continental rods. They hide the inside mount of a colorful fabric roller shade decorated with a serger-finished fabric applique.

To make valances:

1. Cut 2 fabric strips for each valance 2½ times the rod length and 8" wide. Serge the two short ends of each strip. Press under serging and edgestitch.

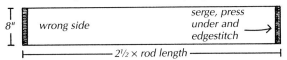

2. With wrong sides together, topstitch 1¼" from both long edges to create rod casing. Roll-edge finish both long edges using decorative thread in the upper looper.

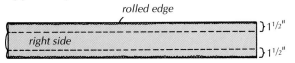

3. Install rod hardware, insert rod into the casing and snap into place!

To make roller shades:

1. For an inside mount, cut fabric and fusible shade backing (see Resource List, page 155) ¼" narrower than inside window dimension and 12" longer than inside window height.

> **PRO TIP:** Make sure fabric is cut on straight of grain or roller shade will not roll or hang straight! Check printed fabrics before purchasing to make sure they are printed on grain.

2. Fuse shade backing fabric to **wrong side** of fabric following manufacturer's directions. Finish both long edges with a balanced 3-thread stitch and decorative thread in upper and lower loopers.

3. Press under ¼", then 1½" at bottom edge. Edgestitch close to top and bottom hem folds to create slat pocket.

4. For applique, cut around a design motif in coordinating fabric, being careful not to cut tight curves—the serger doesn't like them and neither will you! Finish outer edges with balanced 3-thread serging using decorative thread in upper looper.

5. Cut fusible transfer web to match finished applique. Trim 1/16" from outer edge of web, then apply transfer web to wrong side of design. Fuse to shade following manufacturer's directions.

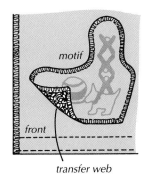

6. Staple shade to roller, insert 1/4"-thick wood slat in hem pocket and install shade in inside-mounted shade brackets.

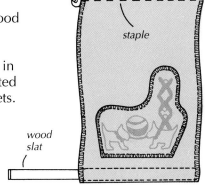

> **QUICK TIP:** For an even easier and faster roller shade, cut fabric and backing 2" wider and 2" longer than needed. Fuse together, then using a straight edge, draw cutting lines for desired shade size. Cut carefully, using a rotary cutter and mat. The shade backing keeps fabric from raveling so no edge treatment is really needed.

3. Basketball Hoop Hamper

Kids of all ages will enjoy slam-dunking dirty clothes into this hoop hamper and Mom will love the help keeping bedrooms tidy. We used a child's plastic basketball hoop, cut our own cardboard backboard, then covered it with fabric. For the "basket" (hamper), we purchased playpen fabric from our local fabric store. If not available, substitute two layers of nylon netting, or Afghan netting from the yarn department.

1. Cut fabric ½" larger all around than backboard cut from sturdy cardboard. Fuse to backboard using transfer web, wrapping excess fabric to back. Cut a second piece of fabric 1/8" smaller all around and fuse to back side, covering raw edges.

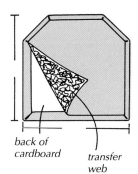

2. Cut fabric 36" long and as wide as hoop circumference, plus 1". Stitch hook half of a Velcro strip to top edge of fabric. Stitch loop half 1½" below hook strip.

3. Right sides together, serge bottom and side, ending serging 4" from top. Use a 4- or 5-thread stitch or reinforce 3-thread serging with a row of straight stitching.

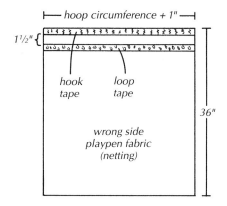
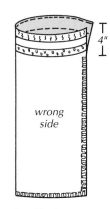

4. Screw hoop and backboard to bed rail, then wrap top edge of hamper bag over hoop and secure with the Velcro.

4. Wall Decals

We love this idea for instant wall decor. Use sharp scissors to cut designs from fabric leftovers, then starch them to the walls. When you're ready to change the room as the child matures, it's a simple task to peel away the decals and wash the walls! Starch designs in place **immediately** after cutting to prevent the "ravelies."

To apply designs, dab liquid starch onto wall where motif will be placed. Dip fabric motif into starch and position over starch on wall. Pat and smooth into place with sponge. Wipe up excess starch immediately. When fabric is dry, wash away "runaway" starch drips.

5. Circus Tent

Children love to play in tents, so we did a quick-change and turned the bunk beds into a colorful circus tent. Medium-weight fabrics like denim or canvas are best for this project. The front panel attaches to the bunk bed and the "big top" to the ceiling.

> **CAUTION!** For safety's sake, fireproof tent fabric, especially if you leave it up at night.

To make the front panel:

1. Cut front panel to fit long side of bed and serge all around with a 3-thread, balanced stitch. We use #8 pearl cotton in the upper and lower loopers.

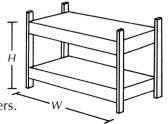

> **PRO TIP:** Test first. Some sergers can't handle pearl cotton in both loopers. If necessary, use it in the upper looper only and use matching serger thread in the lower looper.

2. Stitch 1"x 6" strips of Velcro hook and loop tape to top edge in five places as shown for adjustable "hangers." Center and hang panel on the top side rail using the Velcro strips to secure. Mark size and location of "door" and windows. We centered the door (a slash in fabric), then centered windows on each side, using a dinner plate as template.

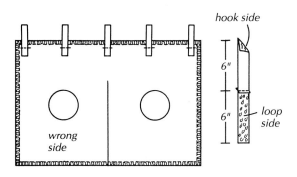

3. Remove panel from bed and cut door and window openings. Serge around the door opening using the same thread and stitch as used in Step 1, above. See how to serge an inside corner, page 144. Serge around window openings. See how to serge circles on page 145. Stitch Velcro dots to tent and opening edges to hold door open.

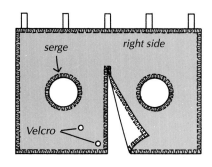

4. For window coverings, cut fabric square 1½" larger all around than window opening. Fuse a fabric design to it using transfer web (following manufacturer's directions), and stitch to tent behind window opening. Fuse fabric cutouts to tent using transfer web.

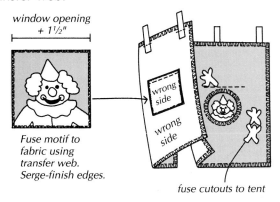

window opening
+ 1½"

Fuse motif to fabric using transfer web. Serge-finish edges.

fuse cutouts to tent

To make the "big top":

1. Cut the big top pieces to fit your bunk bed:

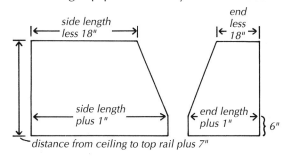

2. Press under and edgestitch ¼" on top edge of end panel. **Right sides together,** serge end to front. Roll-edge finish sides and bottom using pearl cotton in upper looper. Sew a plastic drapery ring to upper corner of end panel. Add window opening.

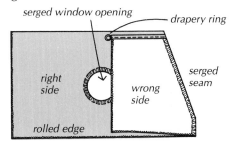

3. Staple top edge of big top front, lapping ¼" over the edge of 1"x 2" common lumber cut the length of the bunk bed, **less** 18". Screw into ceiling with molly bolts, placing it 18" in from the outer edge and end of bed as shown. Screw a cup hook to wall or molding to hold end of big top in place.

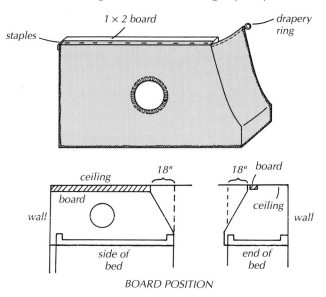

BOARD POSITION

61

Melissa's Playroom

Melissa's playroom is her special hideaway in the attic. The essentially white room begged for color. VIP fabrics to the rescue in bright primaries! Melissa loves playing in her very own teepee and curling up in a plush pillow chair to watch her favorite videos.

1. Toy Storage Wall Hanging

To create the toy storage unit we cut a 44" square piece of backing fabric and made pockets from preprinted 15½" squares, originally intended for quilt blocks.

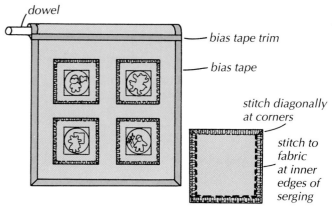

We fused a layer of Textiline (a heavy plastic backing material) to the wrong side of the backing fabric so the unit could support the weight when the pockets are filled. If Textilene is unavailable, substitute one or more layers of shade backing (Resource List, page 155) for the necessary body. The raw edges were bound with bias tape and a casing turned down at the top to form a dowel pocket for hanging.

We interfaced the pockets with shade interfacing and serged all edges with a balanced stitch using Woolly Nylon in the upper looper. Completed pockets were edgestitched to the backing as shown.

NOTE: Use a lighter weight interfacing when using heavier fabrics such as denim for the pockets.

DESIGNER TIP: If you prefer, back hanging with shade interfacing and wrap the completed unit around stretcher bars for hanging.

2. Growth Chart

The preprinted growth chart was interfaced with heavy fusible interfacing and finished with balanced serging, using Wooly Nylon in both loopers. We created a dowel pocket at the top for hanging.

3. Fabric Scarves

Like most children, Melissa loves to play dress-up. She has a great time expressing her creativity by wrapping and tieing fabric in all sorts of colorful combinations. We thought she would enjoy using fabric scarves finished with rolled edges for her

1. Toy storage wall hanging Woolly Nylon balanced stitch on edge of pockets.
2. Growth Chart finished with Woolly Nylon balanced stitch.
3. Fabric scarves with rolled edges.
4. Fabric-covered building blocks.
5. Klaus B. Rau's Teepee with flatlocked sun rays.
6. Puffy sofa made from pillows.
7. Warm Window insulated Roman shades.
8. Window seat cushions.

"designer" clothing—and all manner of other uses that only a child concocts in their dreams! These scarves are each one yard of 45"-wide fabric. Or, use large scraps.

4. Fabric-Covered Blocks

Here's another great way to use up fabric scraps. We covered cardboard blocks (from Lillian Vernon's mail-order catalog) to match the playroom decor! The blocks come flat with creases and perforations for folding. It's easy to cover cardboard blocks or boxes with fabric when you use a transfer web.

> **QUICK TIP:** It's a good idea to practice folding the block before you cover it with fabric.

1. Cut a fabric rectangle slightly larger than outer dimensions of piece to be covered and apply transfer web to the wrong side following manufacturer's directions. Remove the transfer paper.

2. Center fabric, **right side up,** on top of **right side** of cardboard block and fuse center only, following manufacturer's directions. Turn over and slash fabric to all inner corners of cardboard shape so you can wrap excess fabric to back side. Lightly fuse in place, then permanently fuse the entire piece following manufacturer's directions.

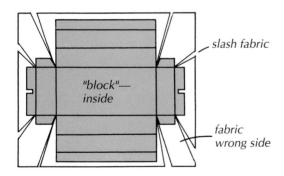

5. Teepee

We love this colorful children's hideaway made from Klaus B. Rau's "My Own Teepee." Why not make one for your favorite little Indians? (See the Resource List on page 155). We followed the pattern instructions, using the serger to speed up the sewing and to add some decorative details. We also used fabric paints to embellish the completed tent with Indian symbols.

1. Serge short edges of pole sleeves and top and bottom edges of teepee with a balanced 3-thread stitch. Use a contrasting color of #8 pearl cotton in upper looper. Also serge-finish zipper opening edges.

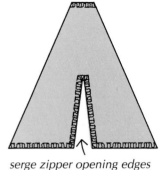

2. For speedy zipper application, use basting tape to hold zipper in place. Stitch in place through decorative serging.

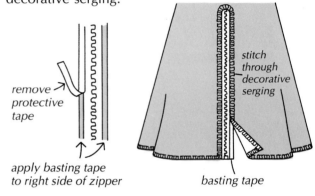

3. Replace sun on tent back with a sunburst window cut from yellow fabric using pattern piece for window frame. Position pattern on tent back and trace inner and outer circle. **Cut out inner circle in both tent and sun applique.**

4. Flatlock sun rays on tent back as shown so inner (long) rays extend 6" beyond "sun" placement line and shorter rays extend 4". **Ladder side** of flatlocking should show on right side. See page 147 for how-tos.

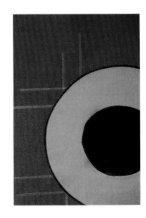

5. Finish outer edge of sun with decorative balanced 3-thread serging. Pin to tent, then serge around opening edges. (See page 145 for serging circles.) Topstitch outer edge in place through serging.

6. Puffy Pillow Sofa

Melissa loves the sofa we made in just her size using four standard bed pillows and one square European bed pillow.

Measure pillows and cut one fabric cover for each, allowing for seam allowances all around, as shown.

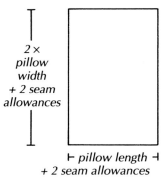

2 × pillow width + 2 seam allowances

⊢ pillow length ⊣
+ 2 seam allowances

For the seat:

1. Stitch 1¼"-wide Velcro on **right side** of the two seat cushion covers as shown. Stitch the hook half of Velcro hook and loop tape to center of one cushion cover as shown. This will be the cover for the top cushion in the completed chair.

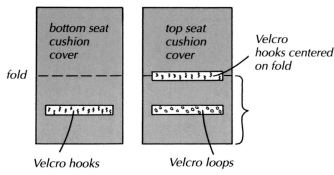

fold

bottom seat cushion cover

top seat cushion cover

Velcro hooks centered on fold

Velcro hooks

Velcro loops

2. With **right sides together**, serge seat covers together on two short sides using a 4- or 5-thread stitch and leaving one long edge open for stuffing. Turn right side out.

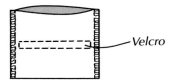

Velcro

3. Center and stitch hook half of 1"-wide Velcro tape over the seam lines at short ends of top cushion seat cover.

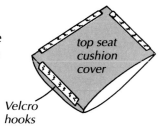

top seat cushion cover

Velcro hooks

4. Insert pillows in seat cushion covers and serge the open edge closed, **wrong sides together**, using a wide balanced stitch with #8 pearl cotton in both loopers. Be careful not to catch pillow in stitching. This is a little tricky, so take your time! Tie off thread chain ends and apply seam sealant.

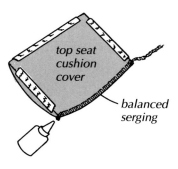

top seat cushion cover

balanced serging

5. For sofa sides and back, stitch the remaining loop half of Velcro pieces to the cushion covers as shown.

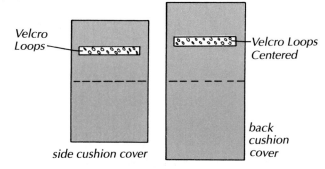

Velcro Loops

Velcro Loops Centered

side cushion cover

back cushion cover

6. Fold **wrong sides together**, and serge sides with pearl cotton. Complete as shown for seat cushions, above.

7. Assemble chair using Velcro strips to secure. Sew ribbons in position as shown and tie corners together.

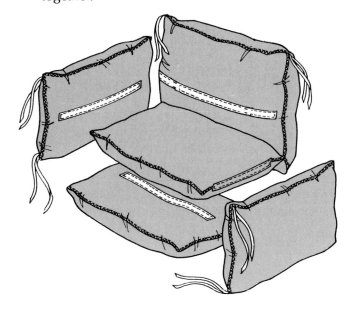

7. Warm Window® Shades

We made the Warm Windows for the playroom using a coordinating fabric from VIP. We decided on an outside mount and due to our mild climate, decided not to use the magnetic strips normally used with this product to seal the windows.

1. For an outside mount, cut fabric the length of the window and frame **plus** 12" and 2" wider than window and frame. Cut Warm Window the **desired finished length**, plus 4" for mounting and the same width as the fabric was cut.

2. Cut top border from fabric coordinate. Finish long edges with decorative rolled-edge stitching. Following manufacturer's apply transfer web to wrong side of border, then apply to shade fabric with border top 4" below top of edge of shade.

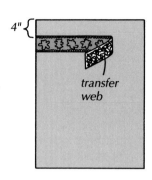

4"

transfer web

3. Pin **wrong side** of Warm Window to **wrong side** of fabric, with top and side edges even. Zigzag stitch close to edges. With a balanced stitch and pearl cotton in upper and lower loopers, serge sides of shade.

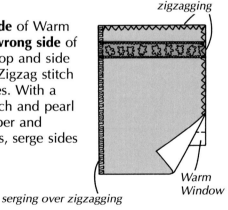

zigzagging

Warm Window

serging over zigzagging

4. Press up a doubled 4"-wide hem at shade bottom, with top edge of hem at the bottom quilting line on Warm Window. Edgestitch.

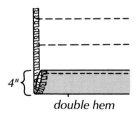

4"

double hem

5. Complete the shades following the steps shown on page 55.

8. Window Seat Cushions

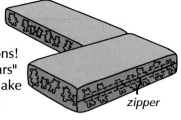

zipper

These window seats begged for comfy cushions! We used the "Tossed Bears" collection from VIP to make them, cutting the boxing strips from a print called "Follow Your Dreams." We constructed the cushions following the steps described for the mattress cover (without welting) in the travel trailer on page 134, but we inserted a zipper in one long boxing strip so the covers can be removed for frequent laundering.

Christmas in the Playroom

Christmas is even more fun when the playroom is decorated, too. Wamsutta's preprinted Christmas fabrics made this Christmas makeover quick and easy.

9. Christmas Tea Setting

For starters we wrapped the window seat cushions and transformed the chairs with fabric drapes finished with decorative rolled edges. For each chair we draped a 1-yard piece and played with tucking and pinning until we liked how it looked. Matching fabric ribbons hold them in place.

The tablecloth is a 1½ yard length of fabric finished with rolled edges. See page 144 for how to turn neat outside corners. We cut the tablemat from the center of a preprinted placemat and serged around it with a balanced stitch using Decor 6 in the upper looper. Double-layer napkins have rolled edges.

10. Draped Windows

What could be easier than adding a simple swag of Christmas fabric to dress up existing window treatments? We pieced two lengths of Wamsutta's Christmas print so the border is at the bottom of both drops. The panel was lined with a coordinating Christmas print and finished with rolled edges using Decor 6 in the upper looper.

To install, we screwed 2"-long screws into the wall at each side of the window and arranged the swag over them. Then we hung ornaments sewn from the Wamsutta collection over the screw heads to hide them.

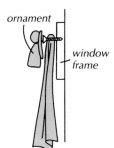

ornament

window frame

11. Fabric Gift Wrapping

In our environmentally-conscious society, what could be better than reusable fabric gift wrap and ribbon? Finish the edges of fabric squares and rectangles with decorative rolled edges or finish with pinking shears. Tie up your packages with fabric strips finished to match.

Serged gift bags are another reusable wrapping, especially appropriate for odd-shaped gifts. We made the large reversible bag to hide a new tricycle using 2½ yards of each of two Wamsutta Christmas prints.

To make reversible bags of any size, fold each piece of fabric, **right sides together**, and serge two sides. Turn one bag right side out, tuck the other bag inside and finish the top edge with a balanced 3-thread

stitch using a decorative thread in both loopers or a rolled edge with decorative thread in the upper looper only. We used Decor 6 rayon thread. See page 145 for how to serge in a circle.

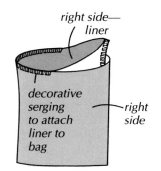

right side— liner

decorative serging to attach liner to bag

right side

We sandwiched a layer of polyester fleece between the front and back of Wamsutta's preprinted gift tags and finished the edges with the same decorative serging as used on the fabric gift bags.

NOTE: It wasn't possible to finish some of the preprinted tags because some corners were too sharp to turn successfully on the serger.

12. Christmas Stockings

Even though there's no fireplace, this makeover wouldn't be complete without coordinated Christmas stockings.

1. Cut preprinted quilted stockings from panel leaving a ½" margin all around. Zigzag just inside the actual cutting line at top edge of each piece to keep layers from shifting while serging. If you have an even feed foot for your machine, use it while zigzagging.

½" extra fabric

2. Adjust thread tensions and stitch length for single layer of quilted fabric. Serge top edge of each stocking, covering zigzagging with a balanced 3-thread stitch. Pin stockings, **wrong sides together**, and zigzag just inside stitching line.

3. Adjust tension for double layer of quilted fabric, then serge together, guiding knife along printed cutting line. We used Decor 6 in the upper and lower looper for pretty coverage on both sides of stocking.

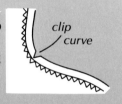

serge over zigzag

PRO TIP: Before serging stocking layers together, clip to stitching line at inside "ankle" curve. While serging inside curve, gently ease fabric into a straight line.

clip curve

PRO TIP: When you begin to serge the two layers together, help the machine over the bump where you must cross previous serging. To do this, hold onto the tail chain to prevent it from curling and getting caught under the presser foot. Then serge just into the fabric, stop with the needle down, raise the presser foot and gently pull on the chain tail to smooth it out. Continue to serge, gently pulling on chain tail as you ease over the bump, then serge as usual.

PRO TIP: Don't try to space the serging stitches too closely—it causes problems with thread build-up. Instead, use a longer stitch length when using Decor 6 or Pearl Cotton for a prettier stitch. Experiment on fabric scraps.

Indoor/Outdoor Play– A Card Table Tent

While attending a local sewing fair, we found this wonderful card table tent pattern designed and sold by a quaint business called *Speedy the Cat, (a Good Friend Company).* (See page 155.)

We made this tent following their pattern directions, but serging the seams instead and finishing the opening, scallops and hems with decorative rolled edges. We also used fabric glue (such as Sobo) to attach serger braid at the roof line for emphasis. To make serger braid, use a decorative thread in the upper looper and a balanced, 3-thread stitch. Serge over 1/8"-wide ribbon.

Sweet Dreams Nursery

Serger heirloom sewing, a quicker "cousin" of French Hand Sewing, takes center stage in this pretty nursery, designed by Lynette's sister, Kelley Salber. We used VIP fabrics and Gosling Tapes to create a cozy nook where a new baby can dream sweet dreams. Whether you're the mother-in-waiting or the doting aunt, you'll enjoy making these lace and ribbon-embellished pieces while you anticipate baby's arrival.

When doing heirloom serging, it's best to embellish the fabric **before** cutting the individual pieces to size for the item you're making.

To make rolled-edge pin tucks, mark tuck locations, press along lines, **wrong sides together**, and serge without cutting the fabric fold. Use decorative thread in the upper looper. We used Decor 6 for all decorative serging in this nursery.

right side

fold

1. Crib Quilt

Kelley created the lace and ribbon-trimmed center panel of the puffy quilt with cream-colored chintz, eyelet trim, ribbon, and entredeux, set off with decorative rolled-edge pin tucks in three colors. Piece the multi-colored quilt border on the serger, using a 5-thread serging stitch, or use a conventional machine.

1. For a finished center panel measuring approximately 23½"x33", follow the diagram, working from center out. Back the center of the finished panel with pink chintz to show through the entredeux.

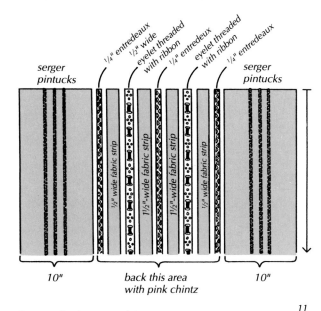

serger pintucks

¼" entredeaux
½" wide eyelet threaded with ribbon
¼" entredeux
eyelet threaded with ribbon
¼" entredeaux

serger pintucks

½" wide fabric strip
1½"-wide fabric strip
1½"-wide fabric strip
½" wide fabric strip

10"   back this area with pink chintz   10"

2. Cut and piece multi-colored chintz border around completed center panel following the numbers in diagram and cutting 4½"-wide lavender strips (A), 3½"-wide pink strips (B), and 2½"-wide blue strips (C).

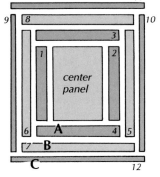

3. Pin quilt batting to blue chintz quilt backing cut to match finished quilt top.

4. Gather 7½ yards of flat lace edging to fit outer edge of quilt top. Machine baste in place.

5. **Right sides together**, pin and stitch quilt top to backing, leaving 9" opening for turning. Turn and slipstitch opening closed.

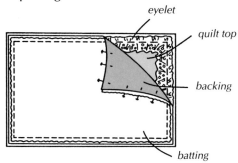

eyelet

quilt top

backing

batting

> **NOTE:** The resulting quilt is soft and puffy. You may want to machine or hand quilt yours by stitching in the well of the piecing seams. See page 37 for machine quilting how-tos.

2. Crib Bumpers

1. Cut each bumper backing and a matching piece of quilt batting the desired finished length and width **plus** ½" seam allowances all around. Cut bumper front, making it 2" wider than desired finished width to allow for pin tucks and seam allowances.

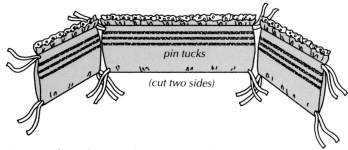

pin tucks

(cut two sides)

2. Mark and serge decorative rolled-edge pin tucks at desired locations on bumper fronts. If necessary, trim bumper fronts to match bumper backs.

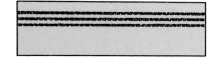

> **QUICK TIP:** Complete all pin tucks in one color before changing threads for the next color.

> **PRO TIP:** To press the pin-tucked fabric without pressing the tucks flat, place fabric, tuck side down, on a fluffy bath towel.

3. For each bumper ruffle, cut a 1½"-wide fabric strip and 2"-wide flat eyelet trim 2½ x the length of each bumper piece. Roll-edge finish ruffle and trim as shown.

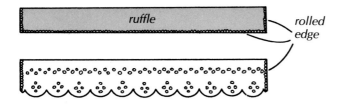

4. With fabric strip on top of eyelet, easestitch together ¼" and ½" from edge. Draw up ease to fit bumper pad front. Pin, **right sides together**, leaving ½" seam allowances extending at both ends.

5. Stitch front to bumper backing, **right sides together**, leaving an opening for turning. Turn and hand sew opening closed. Tack a 20" length of ½"-wide, double-faced satin ribbon to each corner of completed bumpers. Tie bumpers to crib bars.

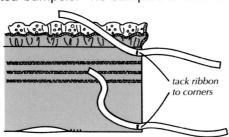

tack ribbon to corners

3. Dust Ruffle

Just a hint of the blue under-ruffle shadows through our eyelet and chintz top ruffle trimmed with narrow blue satin ribbon. Here's how to copy it.

1. Cut muslin dust ruffle platform ½" larger all around than the plywood that supports the mattress.

2. Cut blue chintz under-ruffles for each side of bed, making them the desired finished length from plywood to floor, **plus** ½" and 1½ times as long as each side. Roll-edge finish one long edge and both ends of each ruffle.

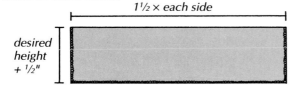

1½ × each side

desired height + ½"

3. For each top ruffle, serge wide eyelet trim to lengths of cream chintz cut wide enough so finished ruffle is same size as its corresponding under-ruffle. Press seam toward chintz.

4. Zigzag narrow blue satin ribbon in place on top of seam using invisible nylon thread in sewing machine needle. Narrow hem ends of ruffle.

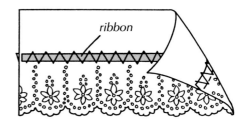

ribbon

5. Layer each top ruffle on its under-ruffle and easestitch ¼" and ½" from raw edge. Pin ruffle to ruffle platform, **right sides together**, drawing up easing to fit. Serge.

4. Crib Sheet

Kelley wanted a crib sheet to match the comforter so we made one using an existing fitted sheet for a pattern. If your mattress is not a standard size or a sheet is not available to copy, here's how to make a custom-fitted sheet.

1. Fit fabric, **wrong side out**, over mattress, allowing for a 3" tuck-under allowance all around.

2. Pin out darts at all four corners to create miters. Remove from mattress and permanently stitch darts. Stitch 1/8" from first stitching. Trim close to second stitching. Finish raw edges with balanced, 3-thread stitch. Mark edge with pins placed 8" on each side of each corner.

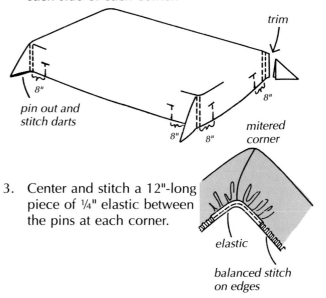

trim

pin out and stitch darts

8"   8"   8"   8"

mitered corner

elastic

balanced stitch on edges

3. Center and stitch a 12"-long piece of ¼" elastic between the pins at each corner.

and start stitching on circles. We tacked rolled-edge chain (page 148) bows to the corners of the square and rectangular pillows.

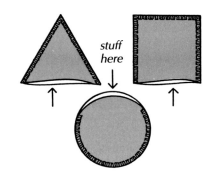

To make a crib pillow to match the quilt, create heirloom fabric pieces for the desired pillow shapes and dimensions. Add ruffled eyelet trim at the ends.

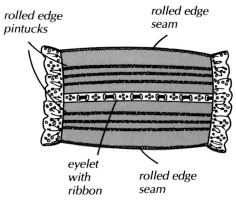

5. Diaper Stacker

Kelley used a commercial pattern for the diaper stacker and made it to match the other nursery accessories by embellishing fabric with heirloom serger sewing.

6. Crib and Throw Pillows

We made a set of geometric throw pillows by serging triangles, circles and squares, **wrong sides together**, with a balanced stitch and decorative thread. For square and triangle, leave one edge open, stuff with polyester fiberfill, then serge remaining edge closed. For circle, leave an opening for stuffing, then complete the serging. See page 145 for how to stop

7. Smocked Pillow

1. Center and stitch a 36" length of Gosling Smocking Tape (see Resource List, page 155) to an 11"x36" strip of cream-colored chintz.

2. Make rolled-edge pin tucks following spacing on diagram.

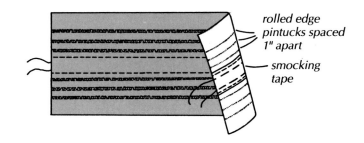

3. Serge finish ends of two 35"-long pieces of flat eyelet trim. Pin to long edges of pin-tucked strip and machine baste in place.

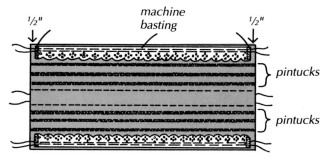

4. Draw up easestitching to fit 11" square of chintz for pillow back. Tie cords, then pull on cords to size—slightly larger than the back so it "poufs up" a bit. Stitch front to back, **right sides together**, leaving one end open. Catch cords in stitching.

5. Press under ½" on open end. Stuff pillow with layers of polyester batting or with polyester fiberfill. Machine edgestitch opening closed.

8. Tissue Box

We used a purchased kit to make the tissue box and transfer web to fuse fabric to the box before assembling. Decorative rolled-edge chain trim (page 148) was attached with fabric glue.

9. Basket

For a custom-fitted basket liner:

1. Tuck fabric into basket, **wrong side out**, and pin to fit inner dimensions. Remove and permanently stitch pinned-out tucks.

2. Make double ruffle as shown for crib bumper, above. Gather to fit basket liner and serge to raw edge.

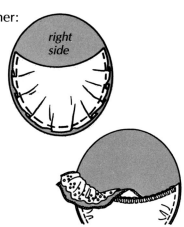

3. Use glue gun to permanently attach liner to basket if desired.

For crisp bows that hold their shape, fuse two strips of fabric together with transfer web (page 155) and finish with decorative rolled edges.

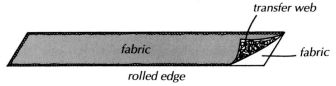

10. Wastebasket

We slipcovered the wastebasket with a tube of fabric, allowing an extra 1½" in the tube length for ¾"-wide casings at the top and bottom edge for ½"-wide elastic. Then we slipped a band of fabric with rolled-edge pin tucks and braid trim over the cover.

11. The Walls

The shirred wainscotting was pieced from the nursery fabrics. The finished piece was three times the length of the wall. To shirr, we stitched over a cord (page 152), then drew up gathers to fit the wall and stapled it in place at the top and bottom edges. Then we stapled a 3"-wide band of pintucked fabric over the top raw edge of the wainscotting. Braid trim glued in place at the band top and bottom and at the bottom edge of wainscotting hides the staples.

12. The Animals

No nursery is complete without cuddly stuffed animals. We used McCall's patterns to make ours, embellishing them with Hollywood trims.

A Country Setting

We created a comfortably cozy country living room in Lynette's home with fabrics from Fabric Traditions, Smocking Tape from Gosling Tapes and Warm Winter insulating lining from Warm Products. The family-worn sofa gained a new life with a simple, unconstructed slipcover. We draped the sofa and wrapped the cushions in durable, washable cotton fabric, perfect for Lynette's growing family.

A smocked window cornice, insulated window blankets, throw pillows and neckroll complete our easy-care country look. These are easy serge 'n sew projects—proof that a change in decorating needn't be difficult, time-consuming or expensive—a real plus for families with young children and limited resources.

1. Draped and Wrapped Sofa

To figure yardage for your sofa, study the diagram. Test your draping ideas and yardage requirements with inexpensive muslin or several old sheets basted together for the sofa. It may be necessary to cut up an old sheet or two to test the wrapping and determine yardage for the cushions.

1. Remove cushions. Drape fabric over sofa and tuck into every crease and crevice. Create pleats in sofa skirt if desired. With fabric positioned on sofa, mark hem with pins or chalk, rounding off corners.

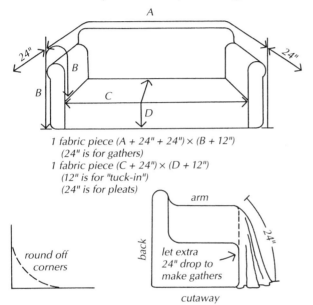

1 fabric piece (A + 24" + 24") × (B + 12")
(24" is for gathers)
1 fabric piece (C + 24") × (D + 12")
(12" is for "tuck-in")
(24" is for pleats)

round off corners

back / arm / let extra 24" drop to make gathers

cutaway

2. Remove fabric from sofa and roll-edge finish along marked hemline. Press.

QUICK TIP: You can use pins or hand basting to anchor some of the draping in position before removing for hemming. That will make it easier to recreate the look you've achieved in the initial draping.

1. Draped and wrapped sofa with rolled-edge finish on hem.
2. Smocked window cornice using Gosling Smocking Tape.
3. Window blankets insulated with Warm Winter and decorative blanket stitch on edges.
4. Aromatic coasters filled with potpourri and serged with balanced stitch around edges.
5. Throw pillows and smocked neck roll using Gosling Smocking Tape.
6. Rocking chair with quilt (see page 77).

3. Drape and tuck cover into sofa, using T-pins to anchor fabric in out-of-the-way places. Wrap fat, decorative cording around sofa arms and back, beginning and ending on inner arms. T-pin in place, then hand stitch to the cover. Add purchased or serger tassels (page 123) if desired.

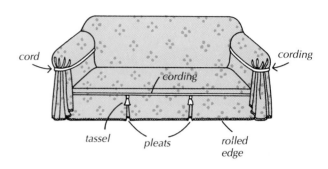

cord / cording / cording

tassel / pleats / rolled edge

4. Wrap cushions in quilt batting, trimming away excess and butting edges together. Catchstitch in place. Then wrap in fabric like a package. Turn under raw edges and slipstitch in place by hand.

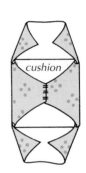

cushion

2. Smocked Window Cornice

Gosling Smocking Tape (page 153) made quick work of this simple cornice. You'll also need two curtain rods to fit each window.

To figure yardage:

1. Decide on desired finished length and double it. (Ours is 8".) Add 1" to this measurement.

2. Multiply window width times 2½ to determine how full to make cornice panel. If you must piece the fabric to get the needed width, don't forget to add in seam allowances. Serge pieces together.

To construct cornice:

1. Serge two short edges on cornice panel, then press under ½" and topstitch.

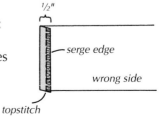

½"
serge edge
wrong side
topstitch

2. Wrong sides together, press under long panel edges so they overlap ½" in center. To create rod pockets, stitch 1¼" from long edges.

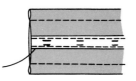

1¼" {
½" {
1¼" {

3. Center Gosling Smocking Tape on wrong side of cornice and edgestitch in place.

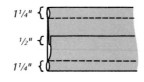

smocking tape

4. Insert drapery rods into rod pockets; mount rods. Knot cords together at each end of tape, then pull until gathers are even and valance fits rod. Tie off cords and invisibly pin to back side of valance so it can be easily flattened for cleaning and pressing.

3. Window Blankets

Window blankets help conserve energy by keeping out cold or hot air, increasing the insulating factor of your windows. We used Warm Winter 1000® (see Resource List, page 155) for insulation in these simple window coverings.

1. Measure window width and height for inside-mounted blanket. Cut fabric, lining and Warm Winter 1000 to match window measurements, **adding 1½" to the width and 3" to the length.**

2. Working on a large, flat surface, sandwich Warm Winter 1000 between fabric and lining. Pin layers together randomly to prevent slippage. Straight stitch, then narrow zigzag all layers together.

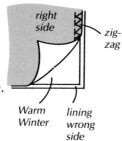

right side
zig-zag
Warm Winter
lining wrong side

3. Decoratively serge the side and bottom edges together using the blanket stitch (page 91) or use a wide, balanced 3-thread stitch with decorative thread in both loopers.

4. For each tie, cut four fabric strips the length of the blanket and 1½" wide. Serge two strips, wrong sides together, using the same decorative serging stitch you used on blankets. Repeat with all strips.

5. With blanket on flat surface, pin mark window length at top. Place a 1"x 2" board cut to fit inside window under shade with front edge along pins. Staple in place at front and back board edges. Trim away excess blanket.

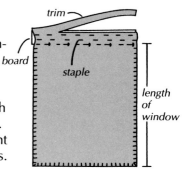

trim
board
staple
length of window

6. Staple sets of ties to board 3" to 6" in from sides.

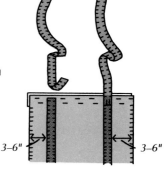

3–6"   3–6"

7. Place board inside window and secure with angle irons as shown.

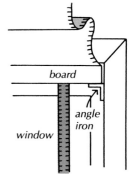

board
angle iron
window

8. Hand roll blanket to desired height and tie, hiding bows on back side.

4. Aromatic Coasters

We filled these coasters with finely ground potpourri to cradle mugs and protect the tables. Hot mugs encourage the release of the pleasant aroma into the room. This is a great gift idea, too!

1. For each coaster, cut two 4½" fabric squares. With wrong sides together, serge 3 sides, using decorative thread in upper and lower loopers. See page 144 for turning neat outside corners.

2. Fill coaster with your favorite potpourri mixture, being careful not to overstuff so mugs can "settle" into the coaster. Pin. Serge fourth side together.

3. Stack and tie completed coasters together with rolled-edge chain. See page 148 for rolled-edge chain how-tos.

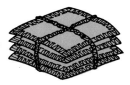

5. Throw Pillows and Smocked Neck Roll

We transformed existing throw pillows with removable pillow covers made from a group of coordinating fabrics. The neck roll illustrates only one of the many clever uses for Gosling Smocking Tape. We know you'll dream up more once you've experimented with it!

For smocked neck roll:

1. Cut 18" x 45" piece of fabric and roll-edge finish the two long sides. Easestitch down center of strip and 4" in from two short ends as shown.

2. Center and stitch Gosling Smocking Tape in place between rows of easestitching as shown.

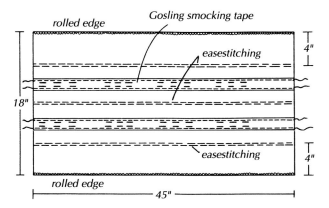

3. Draw up cords in smocking tape to desired finished pillow diameter, drawing up easestitching in center to match.

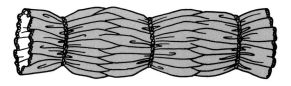

4. Stitch short ends, right sides together. Turn right side out. Roll up a bath towel to fit inside the "smocked" cover.

5. Draw up easestitching to close off ends and tie off threads securely. Tack a 24" length of rolled-edge chain (page 148) to each end and center of pillow. Wrap around pillow and tie securely.

6. A Special Rocking Chair Seat

Lynette's antique rocker sits in the corner by the wood stove, all dressed up in its new finery. We made a new cover using the old one for a pattern. Gosling Folding Tape made it easy to space the pleats. (See the dust ruffle on page 36). We made the lap quilt from scraps using the log cabin instructions in **Quilt in a Day** by Eleanor and William J. Burns. Becky Preston made the adorable doll for us. (See page 155.)

Cleo's Place

Our friend, Cleo, has a flair all her own when it comes to decorating! Her touch certainly shows in our makeover of her dining/living spaces.

New carpeting and paint provide the backdrop for her profuse and eclectic collection of art and accessories.

1. *Window Treatments: Floral cornice and side drapes with De- cor 6 rolled edges. Classic balloon shades.*
2. *Traditional slipcovers.*
3. *Throw pillows with rolled-edge finish on ruffles and wrapped covers.*
4. *Table drapes with rolled-edge finish.*

Concord's fabric coordinates in stripe, floral and moire patterns take on a life beyond traditional in soft balloon shades, padded valances, triple table skirts and piles of pillows. Professionally-made slipcovers for Cleo's tired couch and chairs add the finishing touch. These inviting rooms prove that print mixing can be elegant and sophisticated!

1. Window Treatments

Piped and padded window cornices and shirred side drapes (that don't move) accent the romantic balloon shades at Cleo's windows. For balloon shade how-tos, see page 24.

After installing the balloon shades, we hung simple drapery panels on 16"-long rods mounted at each side of the window. (We cut down the shortest rods available to the size we wanted.) The lined drapery panels were made from one length of 45"-wide fabric with a rod pocket at the top so we could shirr them onto the curtain rod.

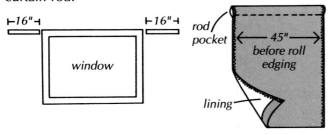

The finishing touch is the padded, tailored cornice which hides the mounting devices for the drapes and shades. First we constructed a wooden cornice from 1"x10" boards, making it long enough to wrap around the drapes and adding a top to fit. The cornice cover was constructed as follows:

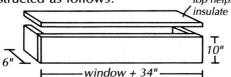

1. Cut the fabric, lining and polyester batting to the desired finished depth, **plus** 3", and long enough to fit around the cornice, **plus** 4".

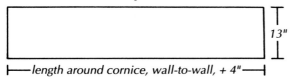

2. Make a sandwich of the three components with the batting inside against the wrong side of fabric and lining. Machine baste fat, purchased or custom-made welting (page 135) to **right side** of one long edge of fabric sandwich. Cut a 3"-wide bias strip of fabric, color-matched to welting, and stitch in place on top of welting, **right sides together**.

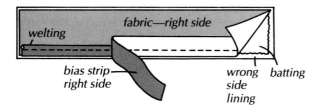

3. Wrap completed cornice cover around wooden cornice, wrapping the bias strip to the inside so welting is at bottom edge. Wrap excess at top over top of cornice. Staple in place. Wrap excess at side to back. Staple.

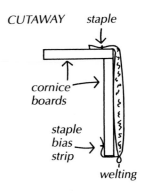

4. Mount cornice on wall with angle irons.

2. Slipcovers

Because there are so many chair and sofa styles available, it would take a whole book to show you how to create custom-fitted slipcovers. We had Cleo's slipcovers made by a professional and suggest you do the same (unless you're already skilled in this area).

Collect magazine pictures of the look you wish to create to share with the pro of your choice. Slipcovers with piped edges will stay in place better and give the look of upholstered styles without the expense. Use ready-made, contrasting piping like that on the wing-back chairs or matching piping as on the striped couch and sofa. Stripes are especially effective and more interesting when cut on the bias for custom-made piping.

For added wear and durability, we had the floral fabric professionally quilted to a polyester batting before making the slipcovers.

3. Throw Pillows

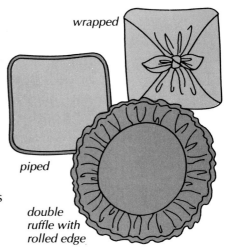

Lots of pillows in assorted shapes and styles make more impact than one lonely pillow tucked at each corner of a sofa. Purchased pillows mingle with custom-made ones as a cozy retreat for Cleo's collection of fabric dolls. We made the pillow covers removable for easy care, following basic directions for the rocking chair cushion back on page 16.

Try single and double ruffles on some pillows and pipe the edges of others. Pillow ruffles are most effective when cut at least 2½ to 3 times fuller than the outer dimension of the pillow. Otherwise, they look too skimpy. If you prefer quick-change pillow covers, roll-edge finish a square of fabric and wrap and tie it around a pillow form.

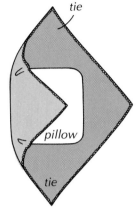

use a contrasting lining for accent— it will show in ties

4. Table Drapes

Cleo says, "If one is good, three is even better!" So, her accent tables are double- and triple-draped for a rich, traditional look. See page 13 for how to cut and piece round tablecloths to fit your table. Hemming them is easier than ever with decorative rolled edges. Purchased lace rounds top off two tables and a square topper completes the third.

We love the mitered striped cloth over the floral cloth finished with fat piping at the bottom to match the window treatment.

PRO TIP: To keep stripes vertical all the way around on round table drapes, gather "skirt" to a circle cut to fit table top (pg. 94).

The Dining Room

With so much fabric everywhere else, Cleo wanted the gleaming wood in her dining room set to show as a counterpoint. A table runner and simple chair cushions were the answer.

5. Table Runner

We made the "mixed media" runner 18" wide and the length of the table plus the desired drop at each end. For a coordinated look, we pieced it from scraps of all the fabrics used in the room. Decorative rolled edges seam the pieces together and finish the outer edges. Experiment with thread colors when working with multi-colored fabric piecing. It may be necessary to change thread colors as you change fabrics for the most effective finish.

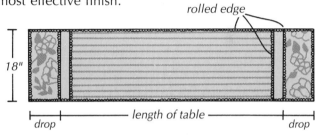

6. Chair Cushions

Cushions with attached "aprons" soften the edges on Cleo's dining room chairs. We love the unexpected change in direction of the stripes at the apron corners.

1. Cut cushion covers to fit size and shape of chair seat. See page 15 for how-tos.

2. For apron, seam strips together cut to desired finished width, plus ¾" for seam and rolled-edge hem. Add an 8"-long insert, cut with stripes in opposite direction, in between the apron sides and front pieces. Finish one long edge with decorative rolled edge. Form 2"-deep box pleats and baste in place.

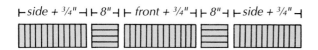
⊢side + ¾"⊣ ⊢8"⊣ ⊢ front + ¾"⊣ ⊢8"⊣ ⊢side + ¾"⊣

roll edge

⊢4"⊣

3. Pin apron to one cushion cover, **right sides together**. Stitch to remaining cushion cover, **right sides together**, leaving opening in back for turning. Turn and add batting or pillow. Whipstitch opening closed.

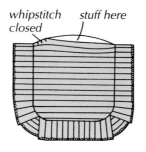
whipstitch closed   stuff here

4. For optional back apron, cut to fit across seat back, making it ¾" wider than front/side apron. Roll-edge finish short ends and one long edge. Finish remaining edge with balanced three-thread serging. Press under ¾" and stitch in place at top of serging.

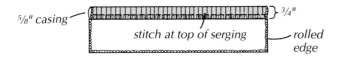
⅝" casing
stitch at top of serging
¾"
rolled edge

5. Cut ½"-wide elastic the length of finished back apron plus 1". Thread through casing. Machine stitch in place with 1" of elastic extending at each end.

1" of elastic   1" of elastic

6. Machine tack elastic to underside of side aprons. Slide completed cushion into place over chair back.

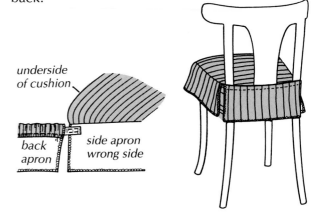
underside of cushion
back apron   side apron wrong side

Don't Forget About Lampshades!

We've shown you lampbase makeovers on pages 91 and 129. Do-it-yourself lampshades are yet another way to add finishing touches to your rooms. In the illustration above, the lamp is simply draped with a square of lace, bordered with fabric "ribbon." Using a pretty, decorative thread, roll-edge seam the fabric to the lace and roll-edge finish the outside edge of the fabric.

It is also easy to make your own pleated, glued, or sewn shades. For easy-to-follow instructions, we recommend the *Instant Interiors* booklet, **Lampshades.** See the Resource List, page 155.

Pillows With All The Trimmings

More pillows! Here the focus is on trims. Victoria Waller from Hollywood Trims worked with us to design these "best-dressed" pillows. All but the bolster were made with envelope openings (page 15). The bolster has a drawstring hidden under the button.

1. This tapestry pillow is finished with self-fabric, flatlocked fringe (page 107). Use decorative thread or glue trim over flatlocking as we did.

2. Trim echoes the metallic accents in the print. Bolster ends are tubes of fabric made from a rectangle 1¼ times the pillow end circumference, and 1" wider than the radius. They were gathered to fit and stitched to pillow cover ends. A drawstring in a casing draws the fullness to the center. Cord was coiled and glued onto a circle of interfaced fabric to create the "button."

3. Our package pillow is SIMPLE! Just tie up a plain pillow with lots of cording.

5. We used Suzanne DeVall's hand-painted handiwork (page 38) on Facile for this posh pillow with Ultra-suede piping.

4. We couched (page 147) a colorful yarn-find onto Facile, then braided more yarn for trim and made the tassels, too (page 123).

6. More wrapping! We trimmed a paisley square with fat braid and tassels and wrapped it around a simple pillow.

7. This gorgeous with a double row a box-pleated ruffle. of trim, baste one to back, then seam top and back together. pillow is framed of Hollywood trim and When using double rows pillow top, one to pillow

83

1. NO-SEW "sculpted" chair cover.
2. NO-SEW wrapped cushion and pillows.
3. NO-SEW window drape— 90" fabric from Spartex.
4. NO-SEW instant slipcover on the love seat—also 90" fabric from Spartex.
5. Hand-painted Ultrasuede pillows.
6. Serged wall-hanging with balanced stitch using decorative thread "find".

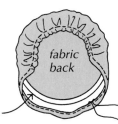

Wrapping Up A Contemporary Space

We transformed this contemporary home in a few hours with our NO-SEW fabric draping and wrapping using Spartex 90"-wide fabrics.

Try it yourself to "dress" your living room in a temporary summer look, as we did, or use festive reds and greens for an instant holiday setting.

1. "Sculpted" Chair Wrap

We started here with a curved-bamboo chair and lots of fabric. We removed the cushion and draped about 4 yards of fabric over the chair. Then we just played. What evolved was a series of tucks that really do stay put. The fabric is not slippery, so even when subjected to the "sit and wiggle" test the tucks stayed in place. A few strategically placed T-pins help hold the front tucks in position.

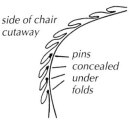

side of chair cutaway

pins concealed under folds

Tuck the bottom edge of the fabric under the bottom of the chair. The fabric across the front is a separate piece that begins under the seat cushion.

To cover the round seat cushion we cut a circle of fabric with a diameter 12" larger than the cushion, serged the raw edge, then turned under and stitched a 1" casing for a drawstring.

For a temporary pillow, this is all that is needed. If you want a more finished look on the underside, cut an additional circle the same diameter as the pillow and insert as shown.

fabric back

cushion

The finishing touch is a shirred cord wrapped under the front of the cushion and pinned in place. Make cord as described on page 86, but cut strip 2½ times desired finished length. To create shirring, gather fabric over cording as you turn it right side out.

2. Wrapped Pillows and Cushion

There's no faster way to transform a room than our quick-change pillow wrap. Our fabric was quite heavy, so we used the "package wrapping" technique:

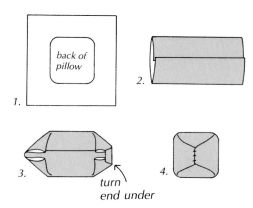

Hand catchstitch to hold in place (or use safety pins for very temporary wrappings).

For lighter fabrics, and another look, the corners can be brought up and tied.

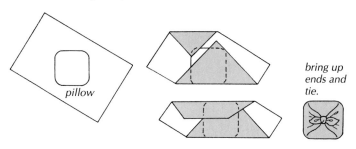

bring up ends and tie.

The knot and tails can be left face up as a decorative element, or turned to the back. (Also see page 81.)

To make the wrapped floor cushion:

We also used the "package wrapping" trick on this huge floor cushion. To make the end result a little more durable we hand sewed the mitered corners.

To make the cording:

Cut a 3"-wide strip of fabric the desired length. We cut ours 14" longer than the perimeter of the cushion so we could tie a fat knot.

catchstitch along edge

QUICK TIP: Make window-drape cording at the same time. Make total length needed, then cut into separate lengths for each project.

Cut fat cording twice as long as your fabric strip. Stitch with fabric, **right sides together**, over cording.

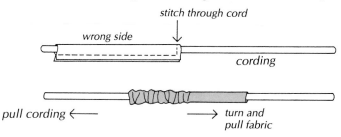

There is no really fast way to turn this right side out. Find a comfortable place to sit and talk with a friend or do it in front of the TV. Enjoy the process!

Trim away excess cord (save it for another, smaller project). Turn under ends and hand sew closed. Wrap cord around cushion, pull tight to give the cushion a "waist" and knot firmly.

3. The Window Drape

This was another "play" project! We ended up with generous swoops of fabric caught up by fat cording held in place with long push pins at the top of the window frames. To start, we measured the distance across the top of the windows and down each side to the floor. We used one length of 90"-wide fabric approximately 4 yards longer than our measurement, and began to experiment with the draping.

1. Begin at one end with fabric puddled on the floor. Bring fabric up to corner of window. Wrap a length of cording (our cord lengths varied from 24"-30") around fabric and pushpin in place at corner of window.

2. Standing on a ladder, continue draping fabric across window top, positioning cording wherever it looks "right," and allowing fabric to drape between cords.

3. Once we positioned the swoops of fabric in a pleasing arrangement, we used our fingers to create and position the gathers, then pinned them to the cording from the back side. (Remember, this is **instant** interiors!)

4. Trim any excess fabric puddling at floor. (We like the look of "excess" but more than a yard or two is probably too much!) Then take your serger to the window and sit on the floor to finish ends with a rolled edge or balanced stitch.

4. Instant Love Seat Slipcover

Once again, 90"-wide fabric (or 120") makes this project a breeze. With the 90" fabric we only needed one piecing seam hidden in the back.

1. Drape and tuck as shown; trim fabric to size. Remove and finish raw edge with rolled edge. Replace on love seat.

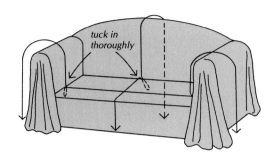

For an alternate slipcover wrapping technique, see page 75. Wrap cushions as shown on page 86.

We kept our draped slipcover simple. With cords, long serger "ribbon" (page 116), or other ties, you can vary the look of the finished slipcover.

"ribbon"

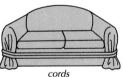

cords

For more easy furniture covering techniques refer to the Instant Interiors booklets (p. 155)

5. Handpainted Ultrasuede Pillows

Textile designer Suzanne DeVall painted the pillow tops. See pages 38-42, 83 and 88 for more of Suzanne's work and techniques.

6. "Serger Art"

Make something just for the fun of it! Linda designed this piece, combining Ultrasuede with a coarsely woven upholstery fabric and some of Suzanne DeVall's painted fabric. The edges of some strips were serged using a balanced stitch and unusual decorative thread Linda found on a huge cone in a yarn shop—there wasn't even a label on it. Other strips were topstitched ¼" from the edge and fringed.

The triangle was cut from Ultrasuede and serged along the edges. A larger piece of the painted fabric was dipped in liquid starch (page 118), scrunched up and left to dry on top of the triangle where it "stuck" like glue (with no visible means of support)!

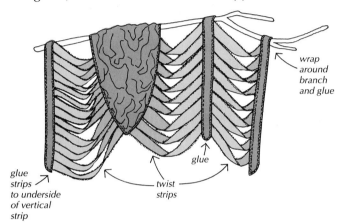

wrap around branch and glue

glue

twist strips

glue strips to underside of vertical strip

Contemporary Living

Look carefully at the rooms on these two pages. They're the same room! What a change you can make with a change in decorating themes! For the room above, we chose very contemporary accessories and details, combining them with existing furniture, a trompe l'oiel folding screen by Portland artist Steven Fuller, and, over the fireplace, one of Suzanne DeVall's abstract canvases. There's not much for you to sew here. Just add dramatic, hand-painted black napkins finished with a rolled edge, and toss a simple pillow of painted Ultraleather onto the

leather couch.
(See pages 38-40 for painting how-to's.)

Eclectic Ethnic

Here we've transformed the room with one of the newest (and oldest) decorating styles. At first glance, it is the "essence of Southwest," but on closer inspection you'll see the rugs are Turkish as are the tiles on the table. The basket on the table is from Kenya. The bundle of twigs on the fireplace IS from a Santa Fe Indian tribe, and of course the branding iron, the boots and the leather draped over the hassock are Southwestern details. Both the painting over the fireplace and the painted table are Suzanne DeVall originals. The folding screen is the backside of the one on the previous page. Our message? For **any** room, the possibilities are almost endless!

89

1. Tab curtains with balanced stitch in pearl cotton; Warm Window Roman shades.
2. "Slipcovered" lamp is wrapped with a circle of fabric finished with a rolled edge of pearl cotton.
3. Blanket throw with serger blanket stitch.
4. Throw pillows—"Serger Waves" with serger tucks in decorative threads; patchwork pillow serged with balanced stitch and decorative thread.

His First Apartment

The hand-me-downs and flea market finds that usually decorate a first apartment don't have to look mismatched, cheap, or out of place. With a little help from Mom, a son's first living space can look colorfully coordinated, (although cluttered with high school mementos and sports gear) for a small investment of time and money. Let him choose the color scheme, then set aside a Saturday to create a cozy blanket throw, easy tab curtains and coordinating pillows like those Marta Alto created for her son, Chris.

1. Tab Curtains and Warm Window Roman Shades

These simplistic curtains were a quick and easy serger project. Just cut fabric and contrasting lining to the desired finished size.

Anyone on a budget will appreciate the energy-saving features of Roman shades insulated with Warm Window thermal lining. (See Resource List, page 155). Follow the manufacturer's directions for assembling. Choose outer fabric to coordinate with the curtains.

1. With wrong sides together, serge over outer edges with a wide, balanced 3-thread stitch, using pearl cotton or other decorative thread in upper **and** lower looper. See page 144 to neatly serge and turn outside corners.

   fabric right side

   lining

2. Cut tabs to desired width and long enough to fit around drapery rod. Finish edges with serging. Pin and stitch in place, positioning one loop even with each outside edge. Space others evenly across top. To pull curtains back, tack a small loop of rolled-edge chain (page 148) at the inside edge of finished curtain. Catch into cup hook screwed into wall.

   loop of rolled edge chain ½ way down

2. Slipcovered Lamp

We disguised a "bargain" lamp from the local thrift shop with fabric wrapped around the mint green base; we roll-edge finished the fabric rounding the corners.

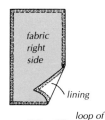

Wrap fabric around lamp base and bind at neck with serged strip.

A strip of roll-edge finished contrasting fabric wraps and ties fabric in place at the lamp neck. To build up a smaller base, consider padding the fabric cover with a layer or two of quilt batting, cut slightly smaller all around than the fabric cover.

3. Blanket Throw

A blanket throw replaces the typical afghan in Chris's room. Cut it from an old blanket or new blanket-like fabric in a size to curl up in for reading or studying. Then serger blanket stitch the edges. This will require testing on fabric scraps.

1. Set your serger for a 3-thread stitch with the longest and the widest stitch possible. (7mm-wide is best.)

2. Tighten both looper tensions and loosen the needle tension until the looper threads run in a straight line along the fabric edge and the needle thread shows on the right **and** wrong side.

> **PRO TIP:** You may need to take the needle thread completely out of the tension disk to loosen it enough. If the lower looper tension isn't tight enough, switch to a texturized nylon thread (such as Woolly Nylon).

4. Throw Pillows

You can't beat throw pillows for an inexpensive way to add a splash of color. Cover old and worn ones with new, removable covers that can be laundered—they'll probably wind up on the floor for TV elbow-propping!

To make a 16"-square "Serger Waves" pillow:

1. For a 16"-square pillow, cut pillow top 17"x27". Using chalk or air-erasable marking pen, draw a line 1½" from left edge of pillow top. Continue drawing lines spaced 1¼" apart across remaining fabric.

   1½ 1¼ 1¼ 1¼

2. Thread serger with decorative thread in upper looper and contrasting color in lower looper. Set for wide (approximately ¼"), balanced, three-thread stitch.

3. Fold and press on first line, **wrong sides together**, and serge, being careful not to cut the fold. Repeat on remaining lines, 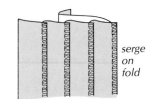 *serge on fold* being sure to begin at same edge of top so decorative thread colors are the same on each side of tucks that form.

4. Mark stitching lines across tucks at the same intervals. Machine stitch across tucks in one direction and reverse stitching 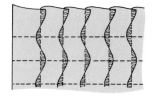 direction on next row to create waves of color.

5. Cut away any excess fabric so finished top measures 17" square. Cut pillow back and assemble pillow as shown for sham backs on page 54.

To make the serger patchwork pillow:

1. Serge 1½"-wide fabric strips together with a wide, balanced decorative stitch to make pillow top of desired size.

2. For padded welting, cut 5"-wide fabric strip to fit around pillow top, plus 1". Pad with a layer of quilt batting. Press under ½" at one end.

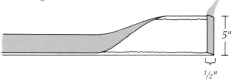

3. Fold welting in half, **wrong sides together**, and pin to pillow top, clipping welting at corners and tucking raw end into folded end as shown. Cut pillow back and assemble pillow cover as shown for pillow sham backs on page 54.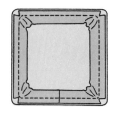

tuck raw edge under

Serger Sampler Quilt

Marta designed this quilt using 19"-square blocks. It includes two blocks that match the throw pillows, plus those described here. (For flatlocking with ladders out and loops out, see page 147.)

1. **Loops-out Flatlocking:** rows spaced 2½" apart; topstitching thread in upper looper.

2. **Ladders-out Flatlocking:** rows spaced 2" apart, ending at random in square; topstitching thread in needle. To begin and end stitching within fabric (not at an edge), release stitches from stitch finger (page 144, step 3 for turning outside corners); position fabric under needle. Stitch desired length, release stitches and fabric from stitch finger and chain off.

3. **Flatlocked corners:** sets of loops-out and ladders-out intersecting corners. Mark stitching fold lines with erasable marker. See page 107 to turn flatlocked corners.

4. **"The Blues":** rows of decorative machine stitching in variegated thread alternating at 2½" intervals with loops-out flatlocking in regular serger thread.

5. **Rolled Edges Galore:** rows and rows of rolled-edge pin tucks (page 70) in various colors.

6. **Swirls:** wavy fabric shapes edge-finished with balanced 3-thread serging in various colors; finished pieces edgestitched to 19" fabric square.

7. **Sampler Block:** combines strips of fabric decorated with serger pin tucks, decorative machine stitching and balanced 3-thread seaming.

After combining blocks to create the quilt top, cut backing fabric and quilt batting to match. Pin layers together and zigzag around outer edge. Decoratively serge with topstitching thread in upper **and** lower looper, using a balanced 3-thread stitch. Tuft quilt (page 25) at corners of each block.

Number 8, serger waves, and number 9, serger patchwork, are described as pillow tops to the left and on the previous page.

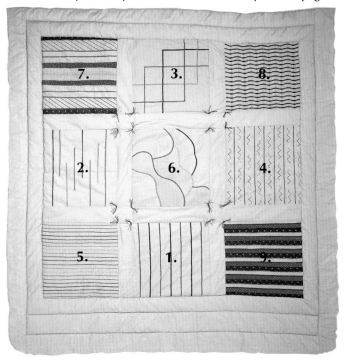

The Sunny Breakfast Room

Houseguests enjoy breakfast in this special breakfast nook. In the summer, this wonderful wicker moves to the veranda (page 136). We loved every print in Fabric Traditions' "Cabana" line so we found a way to use them all in the table and chair coverings. We even made the floorcloth! The table is set with a combination of new majolica and antique Bauerware dishes from Deborah Carnes' collection.

1. Table Skirt

Because we wanted to sew a straight band of stripes to the bottom of the tablecloth, and wanted the stripes to drop straight down from the edge of the table, we constructed it like a skirt, gathering the "skirt" to fit the top circle. The result is beautiful, as pretty alone as with the colorful topper.

side panel gathered to top so we could sew striped border to a straight edge

½" drop to avoid bulk at table rim

3"

1. Table skirt.
2. Table topper and napkins finished with pearl cotton.
3. Chair skirts.
4. Channel-quilted chair cushions.
5. Window seat cushions with mitered borders.
6. Pillows with mitered borders.
7. Window shades using fusible shade backing.
8. Floorcloth.

1. Cut top with diameter equal to tabletop, **plus** 2". Cut skirt 1½-2 times the distance around tabletop.

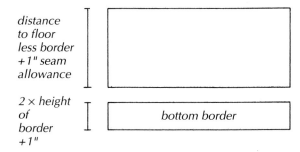

distance to floor less border +1" seam allowance

2 × height of border +1"

bottom border

2. Zigzag over cord for gathering, placing cord next to ½" seamline.

3. Sew short ends of skirt, **right sides together**, to create cylinder. Repeat with bottom border.

4. Fold border strip in half lengthwise, **wrong sides together**. Pin to skirt bottom with raw edges even. Serge together, trimming away seam allowance. Press seam toward skirt.

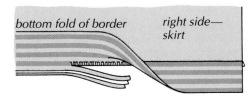

bottom fold of border

right side— skirt

5. Pull on cord to gather top edge of skirt to fit top. Pin, distributing gathers evenly. Serge, trimming away seam allowance.

2. Table Topper and Napkins

This tablecloth is really a collage of "napkins," edges finished with a balanced stitch, then topstitched together onto a liner. The end result is a riot of color, but with continuity of pattern. Design your own topper to use the prints you love, then figure yardage for each. Buy enough fabric for a set of 14" to 18"-square napkins to finish with rolled edges.

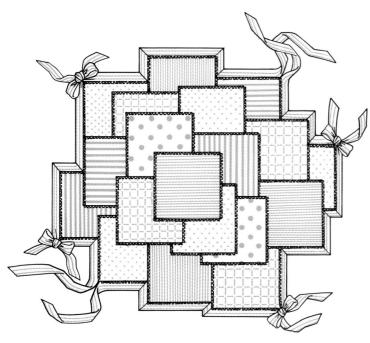

The border is tricky, but we couldn't resist the challenge. We love the look of mitered stripes! Be forewarned—you'll need to experiment a little.

1. Cut striped fabric strips for border twice the desired width, **plus** seam allowances. We cut ours the width of 10 aqua stripes plus seam allowances.)

2. Fold strips in half lengthwise, **wrong sides together**; press. Apply to each section as shown, mitering corners.

Miter inside corners (A) first. See page 35).

Position folded border under serged edges of top and topstitch through all layers.

Sew outside miters (B) or, for ties, fold under seam allowances and topstitch closed (C).

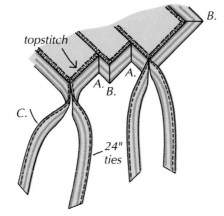

3. Trim the fabric lining to match shape of table topper. Turn under edges and handstitch to underside.

3. Chair Skirts

Since this wicker sometimes lives outdoors in a different guise, we designed this quick-change dressing. Pull-on "skirts" with elastic casings and separate sashes that pull through loops did the trick.

For each skirt:

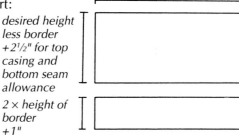

2½–3× circumference of chair

desired height less border +2½" for top casing and bottom seam allowance

2 × height of border +1"

1. Sew short ends of skirt, **right sides together**, to create cylinder. Repeat with border.

2. Fold border in half lengthwise, **wrong sides together**. Press.

3. Serge border to skirt panel, trimming away seam allowance.

4. Press under ½", then 1½" at skirt top. Stitch, leaving a 2" opening.

Cut 1"-wide elastic 3"-5" **shorter** than distance around chair seat to make a snug fit. Thread elastic through casing and stitch to secure.

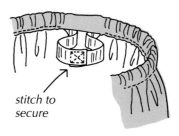

stitch to secure

5. Make 4"-long loops for each chair as shown.

5"

├─2"─┤
cut

Fold under edges.

¾" ¼"

Fold right side over ⅞" and topstitch 2 rows to secure.

⅞"

Turn under ends, position on skirt and stitch in place.

For each sash:

1. Cut two 4"-wide fabric strips 36"-40" longer than the distance around chair seat. Extra is for tieing. (Piece as necessary.)

2. Decoratively serge strips, **wrong sides together**, on all edges with a balanced stitch and variegated pearl cotton in the upper looper. Pull skirt onto chair, thread sash through loops and tie in a big bow.

4. Channel-Quilted Chair Cushions

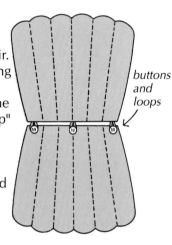

The exact shape will vary, depending on the chair. Make a paper pattern, adding 4"-5" in the cushion width (side to side) and 2"-3" in the length. Without this "take-up" allowance, cushions will "shrink" when stuffed and won't fill the chair. Add ½" seam allowances on top and sides and 2" at the edges where back cushion meets bottom cushion.

buttons and loops

1. Mark channels on pattern, curving the tops. Use a small bowl or saucer to shape curve.

cup

2. Cut two backs and two seats for each chair. Stitch, **right sides together**, as shown. Trim seams, clip curves and turn right side out.

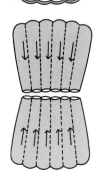

wrong side

wrong side

3. Topstitch along channel lines, stitching from curved edge to bottom opening and ending 1" from raw edge. Backstitch.

4. Stuff channels with polyester fiberfill to desired fullness.

5. Make three button loops for each back cushion following beltloop directions on page 95, but making them half as big.

6. Turn under raw edges, tucking button loops in place between layers on seat back. Hand sew or machine stitch opening closed, anchoring loops securely.

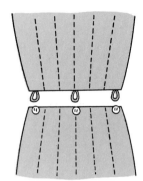

7. Sew buttons on back edge of seat cushion in line with loops on seat back.

8. Button backs to seats and plop completed cushions into chair.

5. Window Seat Cushions

1. Cut three to five layers of batting to desired finished cushion thickness and size.

2. Cut cushion cover top and bottom to fit batting, adding seam allowances all around.

3. Cut striped fabric for border to fit each side of cushion and as wide as you wish, plus seam allowances.

4. Stitch border strips together, mitering corners (page 35.)

5. Stitch mitered border to cushion top as shown.

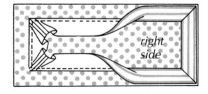

right side

7. Stitch front to back, **right sides together**, leaving an 8" opening in one long side. Turn right side out and insert batting layers. Hand sew opening closed.

6. Pillows

Make smaller versions of the seat cushions, above.

7. Window Shades

These are stationary shades, simply installed using a staple gun. We stiffened the fabric with fusible shade backing. (See Resource List, page 155.)

1. Make a paper pattern the desired finished panel length, **plus** 2" at top for "turn under." It should be 1/2 the window width, **plus** 1".

2. Cut half the panels with the diagonal in one direction, half the other direction. Back with fusible shade backing following manufacturer's directions.

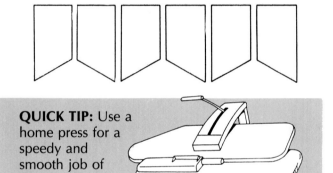

> **QUICK TIP:** Use a home press for a speedy and smooth job of fusing.

3. Cut border strips twice the desired finished depth, **plus** 1" and equal to the width of the shade bottom edge, **plus** 2".

4. Fold border strips in half lengthwise, **wrong sides together**; press. Serge a border to each shade panel, stitching along a stripe and trimming away seam allowances. Press seam toward shade. Trim ends even with sides of shade.

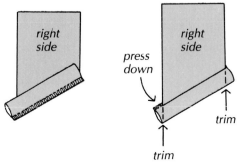

right side

right side

press down

trim

trim

5. Serge sides with decorative balanced, three-thread stitch (or turn under ½"-wide hems and fuse in place with strips of fusible web).

6. Turn under top edge of shade and staple in place inside window frame. Experiment with lengths. We hung the shades at uneven levels for a more interesting and dynamic visual effect.

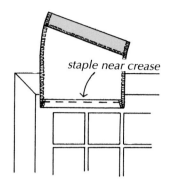

staple near crease

8. Floorcloth

Floorcloths have been used for centuries and are experiencing a revival in Americana decorating schemes. Originally, they were painted canvas. In our contemporary version, patterned fabric provides the "design." We simply coated the fabric with clear acrylic medium to stiffen and finish the surface. Heavy, canvas-like fabrics are best for this technique. We backed this medium-weight fabric with Style-A-Shade fusible shade backing for added body.

1. Cut fabric to desired rug dimensions, piecing as necessary. Press seams open.

2. If using light to medium weight fabric, fuse it to shade backing or to heavyweight fusible interfacing, working with your fabric spread flat on the floor, and protecting floor from iron's heat.

3. Press under 1"-wide hems at raw edges and tuck 3/4"-wide strips of fusible web underneath. Fuse hems in place.

> **QUICK TIP:** To easily cut strips of fusible web, roll yardage loosely first and cut through several layers.

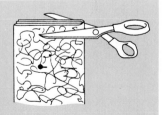

4. Hang cloth in well-ventilated area and coat with clear acrylic. Allow to dry thoroughly. Repeat with at least two more coats of acrylic.

1. SIMPLE tablecloth with silver Candlelight rolled edge.
2. NO-SEW top cloth from Lace Country, decorated with moire fabric ribbon finished with Decor 6 rolled edges.
3. INSTANT napkins with Candlelight rolled edge, plus EASY lace napkin rings.
4. EASY curtains from Lace Country.
5. Quik Trak folding screen.
6. INSTANT, NO-SEW recovered chair seat.

Tea in a Victorian Bay

This dining room transformation in Linda's home went together quickly, evoking a return to Victorian traditions.

1. Tablecloth

Easy! See page 13. We used a rolled edge with silver Candlelight to finish it.

2. Lace Table Topper

This Lace Country 70"-round cloth in the Morning Glories pattern is lovely as is, but Linda couldn't resist an extra, decorative touch, adding shirring and flower clusters in true Victorian style.

1. Place cloth on table. At even intervals around the table, gather lace up to table rim, using a needle threaded with topstitching thread.

Knot to secure. Add silk flower clusters and moire "ribbon" made by finishing strips of moire with a rolled edge using Decor 6.

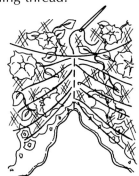

3. Napkins & Napkin Rings

These easy napkins are 16" squares finished with a rolled edge of silver Candlelight. Napkin rings are cylinders of lace slipped over silver rings. Measure circumference of silver ring; cut a strip of lace, adding ½". Serge, turn, slip over ring.

4. Lace Window Curtains

Bay windows with lace...what a nostalgic, romantic image...and so simple to create! Each of the three windows has two panels of Lace Country "Fine Rose," with each panel cut to the floor plus 3" for a top casing. Since the sides are finished as part of the design, the only raw edges are top and bottom.

1. Roll-edge finish top and bottom edges.

2. Turn top under 3". Stitch 1" and 2½" from fold to form casing.

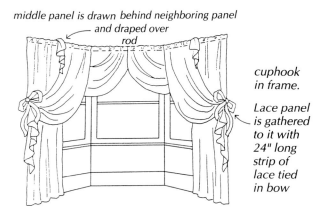

1"
1½"

3. Mount three brass rods 1" down from bay ceiling— one over each window. Keep ends close to each other to visually tie all three windows together.

4. Draw lace panels to sides as shown.

middle panel is drawn behind neighboring panel and draped over rod

cuphook in frame.

Lace panel is gathered to it with 24" long strip of lace tied in bow

5. Quik Trak Folding Screen

The frame is available from Quik Trak, or you can make your own. Stretch moire fabric over it using the techniques on pages 28-29. Linda hung framed photos of her grandmother on it using more moire ribbon.

6. Chair Seat Cover

Many wooden chairs have seats that pop out. For an instant transformation, see page 133.

Instant Table Dressing with Batik and Ultrasuede Scraps

Do you have fabric you just LOVE and plan to make up....someday? Why not convert it into an impromptu, temporary table covering, so you can enjoy it now? Linda just had to have this piece of Indonesian batik. She's not willing to use it permanently as a tablecloth, but it coordinates beautifully with her new teal blue dishes and a pair of Indonesian wooden ducks. Linda loves seeing the surface of her 17th Century plank table and the 1½-yard piece of fabric was the ideal size to allow this when used on the diagonal.

Using Candlelight metallic thread in the upper looper, she finished the raw edges of the batik with balanced serging, repeating the finish on strips of Ultrasuede Facile cut from scraps. The strips cover the selvage edges and also work as napkin "rings." Linda made napkins from fabric in her "stash," too. She has two sergers; one is always set for rolled-edge so the entire table setting was finished in the wink of an eye.

Flatlocking on Linen for Classic Elegance

Barbara Weiland created a beautiful serger flatlocking and weaving technique that works on garments **and** home dec projects. We designed these table linens, inspired by an elegant blouse she made.

Roll-edge finish each piece of linen. Plan length and spacing of flatlocking on paper first. Transfer lines to **wrong side** of linens. For each row of stitching, fold fabric, **right sides together**, on a line and flatlock over fold (page 147) with stitches hanging over the edge. Use decorative thread in needle for decorative ladder on right side. For reversible linens, **also** use decorative thread in the needle. Open out flatlocking, pulling gently to flatten "ladders" against right side of fabric. Then use a tapestry needle to weave Ribbon Floss under and over alternating ladder stitches as shown.

Kite Placemats for a Birthday Party

Lynette designed these colorful kite-shaped placemats with ribbon woven through flatlocking, this time with one row only of stiffer, wider ribbon. We let the kite tails swing up to tie the plastic utensils in place.

Each kite is a different color and the yellow flatlocking and ribbon tie them all together. Add paper plates, napkins, a bunch of helium balloons and a cake...and it's party time!

Plastic-Coated Cotton for No-Sew Placemats

This wipe-clean, ravel-free fabric is the perfect easy-care, table-top fabric. (Use it also in raincoats, totes and other "waterproof" items.)

Just buy and use it for a tablecloth. For placemats it needs additional stability to keep cut edges from curling up. Fuse nonwoven interfacing to the back before cutting into placemats and coasters. We had fun "breaking out" of the rectangular shape, cutting around designs instead of on a straight line.

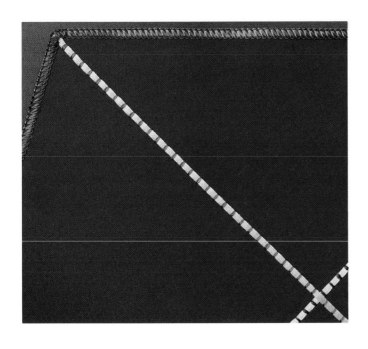

A Country Kitchen

Lynette's country kitchen has a modern yet warm country appeal, featuring lace curtains that don't block her view, patchwork placemats and coordinating napkins and special "cozies" for your coffee mug, buns and casseroles. Wrap up fresh-from-the-oven bread in its very own scarf and you'll set a warm and inviting table with these stitched and serged dining accessories.

1. Country Lace Curtains

If you're looking for a fast finish for windows, consider lace panels like these from Lace Country with rod pocket holes already knit in place. Panels are available in a variety of finished lengths with knit-in design motifs. Choose the one that best fits your windows in your favorite design. Simply cut to fit, do a little serging to finish raw edges, slip onto tension rods and your curtains are finished! How's that for window treatments in an instant? Well, almost!

1. EASY country lace curtains from Lace Country finished with a rolled edge using Decor 6.
2. Kitchen cozies and bread scarf with Decor 6 flatlocking, balanced stitch AND rolled edge.
3. Quilt square placemats serged in Decor 6 with a balanced stitch.
4. FAST and EASY napkins with Decor 6 rolled edge.
5. FAST and EASY chair seat cover.
6. Kitchen towel with iron-on applique and serger trimmed border fabric.

For the cafe curtains, cut two lace panels for each window. Make each panel the width of the window for a shirred look when on the rod. We roll-edge finished the curtain panels with Decor 6 for a beaded look.

NOTE: Cut each panel so it has complete rather than partial rod holes at each end. You may need to adjust the panel widths slightly.

To make pointed valances:

1. Select a coordinating lace panel in an all over design and purchase in width closest to actual desired finished length.

   Cut to match window width, **plus** 2". Fold valance in half and mark cutting line using straight edge and marking pen. Cut.

   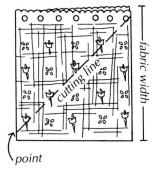

2. Serge flat, scalloped lace trim to valance beginning at top and working to point. Miter bottom point.

   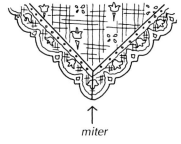

   miter

3. Cut design motifs from lace panels and zigzag to firmly woven cotton. Trim close to zigzagging. Hand or machine stitch to valance.

   zigzag motif to backing fabric

4. Cut panels to fit window and roll-edge finish cut edges.

   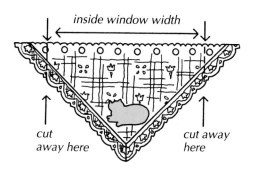

   inside window width

   cut away here *cut away here*

2. Kitchen Cozies and Bread Scarf

Keep your coffee, buns and casseroles under wraps to keep in the heat. Serging makes quick work of these multi-layered "cozies" and adds a decorative touch, too. Practice turning neatly serged corners before you start the actual items. See page 144.

To make a mug cozy:

1. Seam strips of fashion fabric together to fit mug height, then flatlock over seams with Decor 6 in the upper looper.

   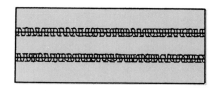

2. Cut flatlocked fabric and backing fabric to fit around mug, plus ½". To keep liquids hot (or cold), sandwich a layer of Warm Winter 1000 between the two fabrics for an insulator. Zigzag the three layers together close to edges.

   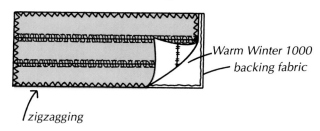

   Warm Winter 1000
   backing fabric
   zigzagging

3. Serge edges with 3-thread, balanced stitch using Decor 6 in upper looper. Stitch Velcro hook and loop tape to short ends for a snug fit.

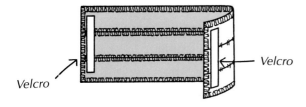

Velcro

Velcro

Velcro

For a casserole cozy to fit a 9"x 13" pan:

1. Cut 13½" x 17½" pieces of fabric, backing and Warm Winter 1000. Zigzag all layers together with Warm Winter sandwiched between the wrong sides of fabric and backing. Serge with decorative thread in upper and lower loopers.

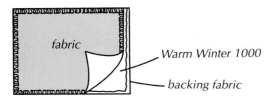

fabric

Warm Winter 1000

backing fabric

2. With decorative thread in both loopers, set machine for rolled edge. Make rolled-edge chain (page 148). Stitch a 6"8" length of chain 2" from each corner of the cozy, backstitching to secure. Knot ends of chain and seal with Fray Check.

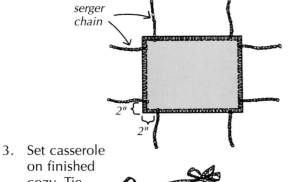

serger chain

2"

2"

3. Set casserole on finished cozy. Tie chains in a bow with double knot.

For the bun cozy:

1. Cut three 13"-diameter circles each from fabric, backing fabric and Warm Window 1000. Sandwich Warm Window between fabric and backing circles; stitch together. Zigzag close to edge. Finish

with 3-thread balanced serging, using decorative thread in upper and lower loopers.

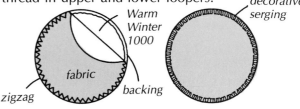

decorative serging

Warm Winter 1000

fabric

zigzag

backing

2. Using Circle A as a guide, mark dotted stitching lines and placement dots (X and Y) on one completed circle. Using Circle B, mark stitching lines to fabric backing side of the second circle.

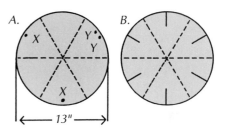

A.

X

Y

Y

X

B.

13"

3. Stitch Velcro hook and loop dots to Circle A with loop half at X's and hook half at Y's. Stitch A to B on stitching lines with backing sides together. Backstitch at beginning and end to secure stitching.

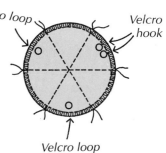

Velcro loop

Velcro hook

Velcro loop

4. Stitch B to C with the fabric sides together and stitch on solid lines, stitching 3" into center of cozy and being careful to keep Circle A free.

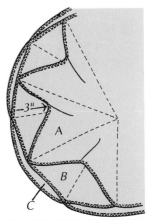

3"

A

B

C

5. Bring Velcro dots together to create pockets.

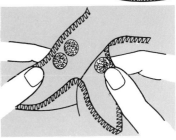

For bread scarves:

Cut fabric to the desired dimensions and finish with rolled edges using decorative thread in the upper looper. We made one scarf 20" square and the other one 13" x 20".

NOTE: Use solid-colored fabric or use two layers of fabric and roll-edge finish with fabrics wrong sides together.

3. Placemats

1. For center panel, cut an 11½" square from fabric A. Cut 1½"-wide strips from fabrics B, C, and D.

2. Working from center out in numbered sequence shown, serge fabrics together, using ¼"-wide seam allowances, to create a 14" square of pieced fabric. Cut backing fabric and quilt batting to match.

3. Pin layers together and bartack each corner of inside panel to keep layers from slipping. Straight stitch ¼" from edge, then zigzag close to edge. Decoratively serge all edges using a 3-thread balanced stitch.

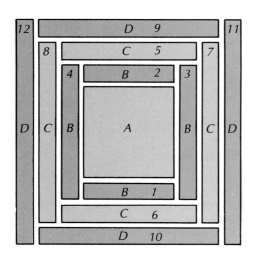

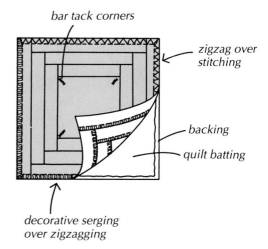

bar tack corners

zigzag over stitching

backing

quilt batting

decorative serging over zigzagging

4. **Optional:**
Machine stitch in
the well of the
pieced seams for
quilted placemats.

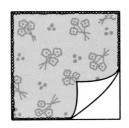

4. Napkins

Durable, reversible nap-
kins are easy and inexpensive
when made on the serger—
and oh, so easy. Cut two
coordinating fabrics into 13"
squares for each napkin.
Layer the fabrics, wrong sides
together, and do a rolled
edge all around with a decorative thread in the upper looper.

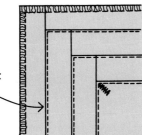

5. Easy Chair Seats

We recovered the antique kitchen chairs by
removing an existing fabric cover to use as pattern for
the new ones. The new covers were wrapped over the
seats and stapled in place along the edge. Braid from
Hollywood Trims was glued over the stapled edges as
a finishing touch, using Sobo glue.

6. Kitchen Towel

Everything in this kitchen has a country touch,
including the dishtowels. We added bands of coordinating fabric and an iron-on transfer to a purchased
towel. Be sure to preshrink the towel and the trim
fabrics to eliminate shrinkage problems later.

Roll-edge serge or
flatlock strips of fabric
together to create the border and finish with decorative rolled edges. Machine
stitch to towel and apply
the iron-on transfer following manufacturer's direc-
tions.

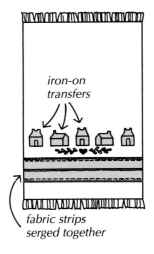

*iron-on
transfers*

*fabric strips
serged together*

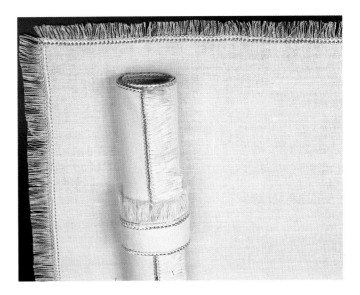

Fringed Placemats and Napkins

We used cream-colored linen and Decor 6 to
create flatlocked fringe on our "Sunday best" placemats
and napkins. Practice turning flatlocked corners first!

For each placemat:

1. Adjust machine for flatlocking with chosen decorative
   thread. Begin with unchained threads (page 146).

2. Cut a 20" square. Pull a thread on each side, 1" from
   cut edge. Fold under one edge along line.

3. Lower needle into folded edge
   at first drawn-thread line. Serge
   with fold halfway between
   knife and needle. Stop stitching
   at drawn-thread line and **carefully** slip fabric off stitch finger
   without pulling slack in
   threads.

4. Carefully open stitching and pull
   flat, at the same time turning under
   next edge along drawn-thread line.
   Flatlock, continuing around placemat.

5. On last edge, stop serging after
   stitching over beginning stitches.
   Remove from stitch finger and pull
   fabric from machine. Tie a knot at
   corner and bury tail chain using
   tapestry needle (page 144).

6. To fringe, pull threads along edges,
   ending at flatlocking.

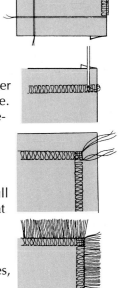

The Italian Country Influence

Linda's kitchen is reminiscent of a cheerful Mediterranean family kitchen, redolent with the aroma of garlic and other Italian spices. Yes, that **is** a cow—a mechanical one rescued from a display at a now defunct museum. There she is, chewing away on a sprig of basil—what else?!

There's lots of room in Linda's kitchen for an expanding collection of cookbooks and cooking tools, as well as an eclectic mix of antique and contemporary furnishings and dishes. The table is set with handmade Italian "Spackleware" dishes from Mamma Ro' (ordering information on page 156), accompanied by their new line of handblown glassware. Creative Home Textiles provided the provincial prints (Torrence Place Collection) that add the finishing touch to this inviting room. The mix and match patterns made designing the room a pure delight.

1. *Valance with balanced and rolled edges in DMC 8 pearl cotton.*
2. *Placemats balance-stitched in DMC 8 pearl cotton; napkins with rolled edge in matching topstitching thread.*
3. *Chair cushions.*
4. *Stool cushions with rolled edge in pearl cotton; rolled-edge cording for ties.*
5. *Potholders with balanced stitch in pearl cotton.*
6. *Jar covers with pearl cotton rolled edges.*

1. Valances

Linda wanted fabric at the windows, but she also wanted light and a view of her garden and terrace (page 140). Flippy, skirt-like valances at the top of the high windows were the perfect solution.

Use a curtain rod like this, mounted 1" outside and slightly above the window frame.

Developing the pattern for the unusual, asymmetrical valance was a challenge. For a 28"-wide window frame enlarge the pattern below. For wider windows, split it in the middle and spread, maintaining an even curve. The finished top should equal the curtain rod length.

width of top of valance

1. For each window, cut a band of fabric the desired width, plus 1" for seam allowances and the exact measurement of curtain rod. Cut matching lining.

2. Make a full-size paper pattern for valance.

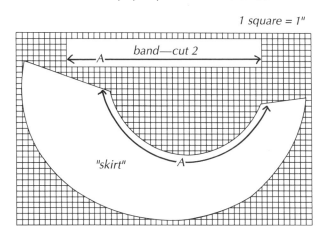

1 square = 1"

band—cut 2

"skirt"

3. Cut out valance. Flip pattern over and cut a contrasting lining.

4. Place band pieces, **right sides together**. Stitch ends, leaving a casing opening. Turn and press.

½"
1½"

109

5. Serge top and bottom edge with wide, balanced stitch using decorative thread.

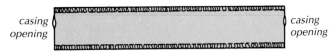

casing opening — casing opening

6. Serge valance and lining, **wrong sides together**, using a rolled edge and decorative thread in the upper looper. Finish all sides.

7. Pin band to top edge, overlapping valance ½". Topstitch along inside edge of serging.

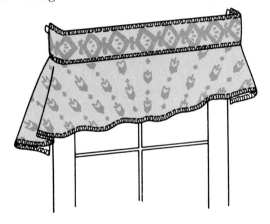

8. Hang the new valance.

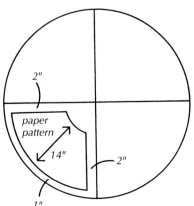

2. Placemats and Napkins

We wanted to create placemats that **really** fit a round table. Here's how:

1. Make a paper pattern, working on the table. Start by dividing the table into fourths.

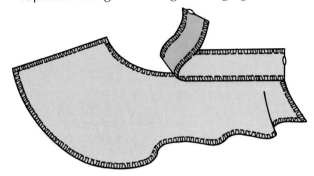

2" · paper pattern · 14" · 2" · 1"

2. For each placemat, cut two layers of fabric and one layer of batting. Sandwich batting between **wrong sides** of fabric. Pin.

3. Serge all around the outside edge with a wide balanced stitch and decorative thread in both loopers (for a reversible placemat).

4. Hand tack every 3"-4" through all layers to secure batting.

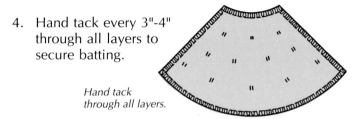

Hand tack through all layers.

The napkins are 14" squares finished with a rolled edge. To keep the look lighter, we used topstitching thread (Mettler Cordonet) that coordinated with pearl cotton used elsewhere.

3. Chair Cushion

These lightly padded, quilted cushions make it easier to linger over Linda's tasty Italian meals! Begin with a paper pattern traced from the chair seat. We wanted a shaped, contrasting border so we made the main pattern pieces smaller. Don't forget to allow for seams around the cushion cover **and** the border strip.

paper pattern

1. Cut top and bottom. Cut border strip 2 times desired finished width, plus 1" for seams. Cut long enough to fit around outer edge of cushion cover.

2. Mark and miter corners on border strip.

90°

3. Sew border to cushion top, **right sides together** Trim seam allowances.

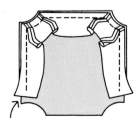 

Angle strip out so stitching finishes in center of strip. Stop ½" from end of strip.

4. Make four ties for each cushion. Sew, **right sides together**, angling at one end.

Trim seam allowances; turn and press.

5. Baste ties to **right side** of cushion back. Stitch back to remaining raw edge of border strip between ties, then stitch front and back to each other beyond ties as shown. Leave opening for turning.

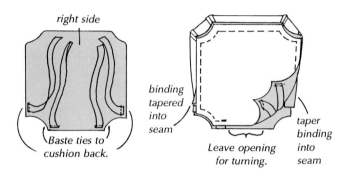

right side

Baste ties to cushion back.

binding tapered into seam

Leave opening for turning.

taper binding into seam

6. Clip corners, trim seam allowances, turn and press.

7. Trace around finished cover on top layer of 2 or 3 layers of polyester batting. Cut out shape and insert in cover through opening. Slipstitch opening at ends of border and across back of cushion cover.

Insert batting then slipstitch.

8. Hand tack quilt layers together. (We used the print pattern as guide for stitch placement.)

4. Stool Cushions

1. Measure the diameter of the stool seat and order 2" thick foam cut to size from a foam supplier. Check Yellow Pages of your phone book.

2. Cut a top circle, adding ½" seam allowances. Cut bottom in two pieces, adding zipper seam allowance. (See page 35.) Cut a 3"-wide boxing strip for sides, equal to the circumference of the finished pillow, plus seam allowances.

3. Insert zipper in back. (See page 35.)

4. Sew boxing strip into a cylinder.

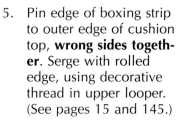

5. Pin edge of boxing strip to outer edge of cushion top, **wrong sides together**. Serge with rolled edge, using decorative thread in upper looper. (See pages 15 and 145.)

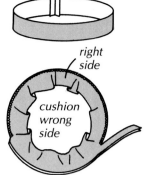

right side

cushion wrong side

Repeat for bottom circle. Insert foam cushion.

6. Make extra rolled-edge chain (page 148) for ties. For each tie, thread 16" of chain through tapestry needle. Position cushion on stool. Pull chain through cushion on underside, in line with stool leg. Knot at cushion and at each end. Repeat for each leg.

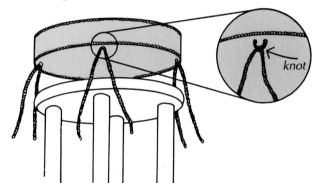

knot

5. Pot Holders

Some are square. Some follow the shape of the fabric. Make like placemats, except at one corner leave one long serger tail to tie onto wooden ring.

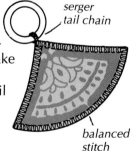

serger tail chain

balanced stitch

6. Jar Covers

Each is a single thickness of fabric with rolled edges. See pages 15 and 145 for serging a circle. Cut circle 3"-4" larger than jar lid diameter. Fasten with a rubber band, then wind rolled-edge chain (pg 148) over band. Tie in bow.

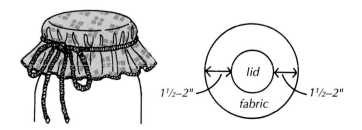

1½–2" lid 1½–2"

fabric

Christmas in the Living Room

The inviting glow of a Yule log draws you to this elegant Victorian Christmas setting in this turn-of-the-century living room. Concord Fabrics' Printed Christmas panels made easy work of simple-to-serge yet stunning results. Golden-winged cherubs and angels alight in the twinkling tree and stand watch at the traditional evergreen wreath dressed up in dried roses and hydrangea blossoms. Full-blown Victorian roses adorn the tree skirt, stockings and pillow, continuing the theme. An antique wagon, heirloom dolls, family photos and glowing candles complete this picture-perfect, fireside setting.

The Draped Mantel

We draped the mantel in an 18"-wide strip of chintz finished with rolled edges in Decor 6 for added sheen. Twist, tie and tack the swath of fabric ribbon to the mantel, then add tassel-trimmed Christmas stockings. By making your own serger-chain tassels you can perfectly color-coordinate them to your project.

1. Cut stockings from printed panels; interface with fusible interfacing. Serge top edges with decorative thread in upper and lower loopers, using a balanced three-thread stitch. Layer front and back, **wrong sides together**, and serge outer edges, trimming away excess seam allowance. Tie off thread chains; apply Fray Check seam sealant to knots.

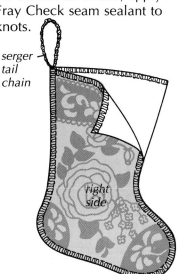

serger tail chain

right side

2. Make 3 rolled-edge chain tassels for each stocking (page 123) and hand tack in place. Add rolled-edge chain hanging loop if desired.

Angels, Tree Skirt and Pillow

The angels and cherubs were cut from printed panels and constructed on the sewing machine following the directions printed on the fabric. Cut the tree skirt from the preprinted panel and roll-edge finish with decorative thread in the upper looper.

We used Concord's preprinted tablecloth for a pillow cover instead. Rather than following the printed, curved border, we roll-edge finished the fabric with straight edges, then simply wrapped an existing pillow in the fabric—a great, quick-change trick for seasonal decorating.

An Elegant Christmas Dinner

Who could resist a holiday dinner set at this table in traditional Christmas reds and greens interwoven with the golden highlights of tissue lame and decorative metallic serger accents? The bountiful feast soon to come is heralded with brass horns tucked into a lush centerpiece of fresh fruit and glistening foliage, all intertwined with coordinating ribbon. Concord Fabrics' coordinated group of Christmas prints provided the inspiration for this elegant and opulent setting.

Tablecloth, Placemats and Napkins

The attached ruffle on the rich paisley table covering creates the illusion of two tablecloths—a great way to stretch the holiday budget. Two-in-one napkin squares reverse to a coordinating print and, when tucked into miniature brass horn ornaments, add holiday sparkle to the bold red table settings.

The napkins also double as placemats, draped over the table for a dramatic new twist on table dressing.

For each napkin/placemat combo, cut and layer two 15" fabric squares, **wrong sides together**. Finish with a rolled edge using Candlelight metallic thread in the upper looper. To avoid thread pokeys, reverse fabric grainline as shown with arrows.

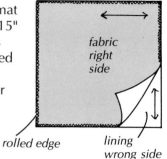

fabric right side

rolled edge   lining wrong side

For the ruffled tablecloth, first measure the table and decide on finished tablecloth size and ruffle width. The bottom edge of our ruffle just brushes the chair cushions. For a more opulent look, you may want it to drop to the floor.

1. Tablecloth with attached ruffle and decorative balanced stitch using gold Candlelight thread.
2. EASY reversible napkin/placemat combo finished with rolled edges in gold Candlelight.
3. EASY fabric ribbons with balanced stitch finish in gold Candlelight.
4. Beautiful large bows with rolled-edge finish using milliner's wire for shaping.

Dinnerware is from Mamma Ro'. For ordering information, see page 156.

Measure table and desired drop:

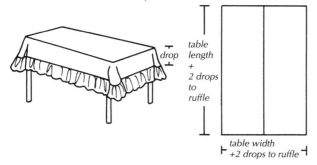

table length + 2 drops to ruffle

drop

table width +2 drops to ruffle

1. Cut the tablecloth, piecing as needed to create the desired size. We pieced down the center since the centerpiece would hide most of the piecing seam. Also refer to page 150. Be sure to match print pattern when seaming.

2. If table has curved outer edges and you want finished cloth to hang evenly all around, curve outer corners of fabric to match. To make a pattern for table curve, lay a piece of paper over table corner and crease around curve with palm of hand.

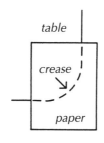

table

crease

paper

3. Finish cloth with a balanced, 3-thread stitch using Candlelight metallic thread in the upper looper and a tan or gold-colored thread that blends with it in needle and lower looper.

4. Cut ruffle the desired width and 2 to 3 times the outer measurement of tablecloth. Piece strips as needed and join ends with serged seams. Roll-edge finish one edge with Candlelight in upper looper. Serge finish remaining edge to control ravelling in laundering.

5. On **wrong side** of ruffle, zigzag over cord placed next to seamline on one long edge. To guide you in attaching ruffle so fabric gathers evenly, divide and mark tablecloth and ruffle as shown.

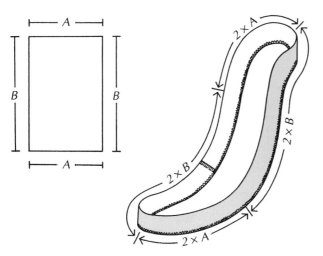

A

B

A

2 × A

2 × B

2 × B

2 × A

6. Pin ruffle to tablecloth matching marks with **right side of ruffle next to wrong side of tablecloth and finished edge of cloth overlapping top edge of ruffle 1"**. Pull on cord to gather ruffle to fit. Pin securely. Topstitch, placing stitching just above metallic serging.

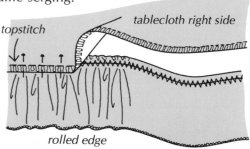

topstitch

tablecloth right side

rolled edge

Beautiful Ribbons and Bows

A hunter's horn continues our theme at the fireplace, trimmed with a bow of paisley and gold tissue lame. We "animated" the bow and the matching tree topper by roll-edge finishing the fabric layers with Candlelight, serging over craft or florist's wire so we could give a little life to the finished bows. We used transfer web to fuse the fabric strips together before serging to prevent slippage and add body.

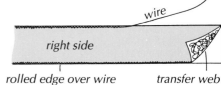

wire

right side

rolled edge over wire

transfer web

The smaller bows on the tree, and the ribbons wound throughout the centerpiece, are 2½"-wide fabric strips serged with a balanced stitch using the same gold Candlelight in both loopers. Here, for a softer look, we did not use the wire. For added body, spray starch the finished bows.

Add the twinkle of hundreds of tiny lights and a glowing fire to bid a festive welcome to all who will partake of this holiday celebration.

The Guestroom/Office

An unexpected, opulent blend of colors and fabrics creates a warm, inviting mood in this guest room/office where Barbara Weiland greets her color and wardrobe clients and houses occasional out-of-town guests. A small, empty room with odd angles and warm apricot walls that couldn't be changed (she rents the house) provided the decorating challenge.

Antique-sleuthing turned up a wonderful array of furniture—a Victorian daybed, a Eurasian walnut dressing table and chair, a Chinese red trunk (for linen storage), wicker rocker and basket, and an oak dressing screen. The daybed does double-duty as a sofa and creates the focal point between two dramatically draped windows. A splendid collection of colorful

117

prints from VIP in exotic shades of red, green and apricot on a black ground pull all the pieces together, creating a rich look that male guests appreciate too.

Rolled edges take center stage—on pillows, coverlet, curtains and chair covers. Even the metallic-sparked red tassels used on pillows, tiebacks and custom-made bolsters are made with rolled-edge chain. The border at ceiling level is simply a "stripe" cut from the drapery fabric, serger finished and starched to the wall. Guests will appreciate the thoughtfully supplied basket of serger-trimmed towels to carry to the bath.

1. *Starched fabric borders with decorative balanced serging on edges.*
2. *Daybed coverlet.*
3. *Daybed dust ruffle with rolled-edge finish.*
4. *Angled valance with attached drape, rolled-edge finish.*
5. *Draped pillow tied with serger finished fabric bow.*
6. *Pillowcase pillows with rolled-edge finish.*
7. *Flatlock patchwork pillow.*
8. *Knife-edge rocker cushion with rolled-edge ruffle.*
9. *Terrific mixed-thread serger tassels on bolster.*
10. *EASY chair-back cover and seat with rolled-edge finish.*
11. *Antique dressing screen panels with rolled-edge finish.*
12. *Pleated ruffle for drapery tiebacks and towel trim.*
13. *EASY fabric-covered file box.*
14. *Candlestick lamp.*

1. Fabric Borders

With a rotary cutter, mat and ruler, we cut the fabric border from the floral stripe coordinate, using the wider of the two "stripes" for the most impact. Raw edges were serged with Decor 6 using a wide, closely spaced, balanced 3-thread stitch for the most coverage and visibility.

To conserve yardage, the border was pieced from strips of fabric, each cut several inches longer than the longest wall, allowing for pattern matching. It was serged, then smoothed into place at ceiling level using liquid starch as the "glue" (a technique developed by Judy Lindahl—see page 159). Liquid starch is blue but it dries without noticeably affecting fabric color. When ready to change your decor, it's easy to pull the fabric off, wash away the starch, and proceed with a new treatment. It's the perfect solution for adding the look of wallpaper to temporary living situations—apartments and dorm rooms—for example.

1. To piece the border, use narrow seams; match pattern carefully. Press seams open, cutting the ends at an angle.

match

cut the
ends at an angle

2. Finish edges with wide, closely spaced, balanced serging. Cut off serger tails and apply Fray Check liberally.

To apply borders:

1. Place plastic drop cloths on the floor to catch drips—liquid starch is "runny".

sponge paint brush

2. Begin in the least conspicuous corner of the room. Apply starch to wall with sponge paintbrush. A 6" to 10"-long swath of starch is most manageable.

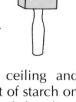

3. Position border with one edge at ceiling and smooth onto starch. Apply a thin coat of starch on top of border. Continue smoothing with hands or small sponge. Push pin border in place to hold while drying. Continue around room and cut away excess border when you reach starting point. Allow to dry; remove pins.

4. Keep a damp sponge handy to wipe up starch drips as you go. It takes less time and "muscle power" to remove starch while wet!

2. Daybed Coverlet

The colorful daybed coverlet is lined with a coordinating print and trimmed with three ruffles in graduated sizes. Cutaway corners fit around the bed frame.

First create a piece of fabric large enough to cover and drop over the sides and ends to the bottom edge of the mattress, plus ½" all around for seam allowances. Size depends on the mattress and varies, particularly with antique furniture.

piecing seams

one-fabric width

If you must piece the coverlet, cut center panel from a full width of fabric and piece the remaining width in equal amounts on each side of center panel. Be sure to match pattern repeats. Repeat with lining.

Calculate ruffle widths so bottom ruffle ends just past the bottom edge of side rail. Don't forget seam allowances on one edge of each ruffle and cut ruffles 2½ to 3 times fuller than the finished length of each edge of the coverlet.

To assemble coverlet:

1. Cut away squares at each corner of coverlet and lining to fit around bed frame. Each side of square equals length of drop from top to bottom edge of mattress, **LESS** ½".

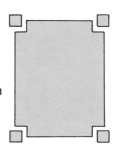

2. Roll-edge finish one long edge and two short ends of each ruffle. Stack ruffles with remaining raw edges even and easestitch ½" and ¼" from edge.

rolled edge

3. Pin ruffles to edges of coverlet between the ½" seam allowances at corners. Draw up easestitching to fit and distribute gathers evenly. Machine baste.

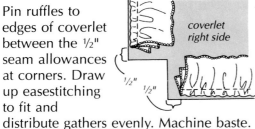

coverlet right side

½" ½"

4. Right sides together, stitch lining to coverlet. Leave 12" opening for turning. Turn; press; hand sew opening closed.

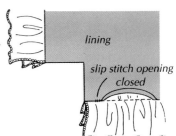

lining

slip stitch opening closed

3. Daybed Dust Ruffle

Making a standard dust ruffle for this antique daybed presented a creative challenge. Because the box spring rests on slats, it was impossible to drop the ruffle **between** the box spring and the side rails. The box spring also sits well below the top edge of the side rail, so the ruffle couldn't go **over** the rail either. Barbara's solution—a 3-piece dust ruffle.

1. For ruffle "platform," cut muslin or sheeting the width of box spring and the length of box spring, plus 1" for seams. Finish long edges with balanced 3-thread serging stitch.

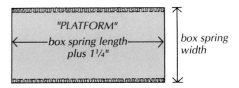

"PLATFORM"
box spring length plus 1¼"
box spring width

2. Cut end ruffles 2½ to 3 times box spring width and the length from top of box spring to floor, plus ½" for seam. Roll-edge finish one long edge and short ends of each ruffle. Easestitch ¼" and ½" from raw edge.

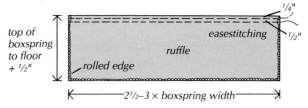

top of boxspring to floor + ½"

rolled edge

ruffle

easestitching

¼"
½"

2½–3 × boxspring width

3. Pin a ruffle to each end, drawing up easestitching to fit. Distribute gathers evenly. Machine stitch, then serge through all layers to finish seam.

dust ruffle platform

stitch by machine

serge to finish

4. Cut each side ruffle 2½ to 3 times the length of the box spring and the length from the **bottom** edge of side rail to floor plus 1". Roll-edge finish and easestitch as shown for end ruffles.

5. For each side ruffle cut a 3"-wide ruffle band as long as inner length of side rail from post to post, plus ½". Serge finish two short ends and one long edge of band.

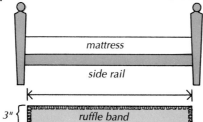

mattress

side rail

3" { ruffle band

6. Pin and stitch ruffle to remaining raw edge of band, drawing up to fit and distributing gathers evenly. Press under 1½" of band, pin and stitch in the ditch from right side. Edgestitch ends.

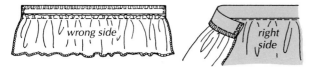

wrong side

right side

7. Staple or thumbtack ruffle band to inside of side rail, adjusting so bottom edge of ruffle hangs just above floor level. Or use Velcro as shown on page 27. Assemble bed with ruffle platform between mattress and box spring.

staple

inside of rail

4. Angled Valance With Attached Drape

Barbara wanted continental rods for the angled valance over the drapes but without the expense of two rods at each window. We solved the problem by attaching the lined valance to the completed drapery panel with the casing stitching.

Make lined or unlined drapery panels 2½ to 3 times the window width, including the woodwork. **Finished, hemmed** panels are the desired finished length from top of rod, plus 2" for self-ruffle above the rod. Roll-edge finish top edge of finished panel.

To make the angled, lined valance:

1. Make a scale drawing of window on ¼" graph paper. Sketch in drapery panel with tieback.

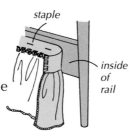

tissue overlay

2. On tracing paper overlays, sketch in valances. For best

visual balance, longest edge is about 1/3 the finished length of drape. Shorter edge is about 10" shorter. Make several tracings, sketching various valance sizes until you see one that is visually appealing. Determine finished lengths for the two sides of panel based on sketch.

3. Cut and piece valance panel the same measurement across top as the **finished** drapery panel plus 1". Cut it the depth of the longest side of selected valance size **plus** 2" for top self-ruffle. Mark length of short side of valance on one edge and draw in the angle. Cut on the line. Repeat with valance lining.

finished drapery panel + 1"

4. **Right sides together**, stitch valance to lining at sides. Turn and press. Roll-edge finish top and bottom valance edges.

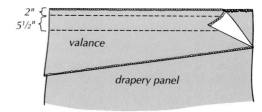

rolled edges

5. Pin valance to drapery panel. Stitch 2" from top edge and again 5½" below first stitching to form casing for a 4½"-wide continental rod. (Adjust casing size if needed to fit narrower or wider rods.)

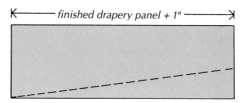

2"
5½"

valance

drapery panel

6. Slip rod through casing created between drapery and valance and mount rod on wall brackets. Pull layers apart above rod for a double ruffled effect.

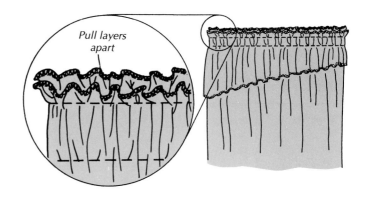

Pull layers apart

5. Draped and Tied Pillow

All tied up in a "bow," these unique pillow covers aren't as complicated as they look. We used a coordinating print for a "drape" caught in the pillow cover seams, then scrunched and tied it with a serger-finished fabric bow made from a third print. Tassels make good ties, too!

For a 14"-square removable pillow cover:

1. Cut 15"-square pillow front; cut and prepare pillow back following pillow sham directions on page 54.

2. Cut the drape as shown in diagram. Staystitch short edges of "drape"; roll-edge finish long edges, skimming edge with serger knife as you stitch.

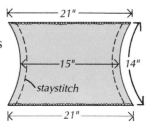

3. Pin and stitch to pillow front, clipping curve as needed.

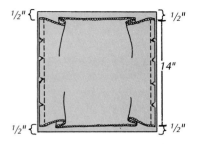

4. Attach pillow back following directions on page 54, using ½"-wide seam allowances.

5. For tie, layer two 2"x 45" fabric strips with bias-cut ends, **wrong sides together**; roll-edge finish all around. Wrap around drape, drawing into center of pillow and tie in bow.

6. Pillowcase Pillows

Here's a clever way to solve the "extra pillow storage problem!" Pop plump bed pillows into decorator pillowcases tied up with roll-edge-finished, double-faced fabric ribbons. Guests remove pillows at bedtime, then hide them away in the morning.

Cut the cases the actual length of the pillow and finish with a 12"-wide lined band of coordinating fabric. Measure a pillowcase for the finished width, double it and add seam allowances.

1. Fold pillowcase and band fabrics in half, right sides together. Serge as shown.

band   band
        lining

pillowcase

2. Tuck band, lining, inside band, **wrong sides together**; roll-edge finish one edge.

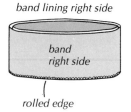

band lining right side

band right side

rolled edge

3. Pin band to wrong side of pillowcase, raw edges even. Roll-edge seam. Turn right side out.

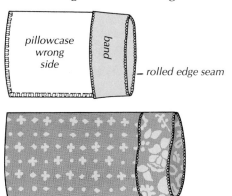

pillowcase wrong side

band

— rolled edge seam

4. Pop pillow inside and tie with a 2"x 60" double-faced ribbon. Cut ribbon ends on angle before finishing with rolled edges.

7. Flatlock Patchwork Pillow

Piece random scraps of fabric together with decorative flatlocking.

Since pillows often get a lot of handling, topstitch through the center of the flatlocking to hold the loops down securely so they're less likely to catch or snag. Use for a pillow top.

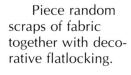

topstitch

8. Knife-Edge Rocker Cushion

To add a rolled-edge ruffle to the rocker cushion cover, we made it ½" larger all around than the desired finished size. (To determine custom-made cushion size for chair seats, see rocking chair cushion, page 9.)

1. Stitch front and back cushion covers, **wrong sides together**, leaving opening across back. Turn and press, pressing under opening edges.

2. Roll-edge finish outer edges of cushion, **being careful not to cut the cover**. Begin and end rolled edge at opening ends. Machine stitch ½" from rolled edges, backstitching at beginning and end.

3. Roll-edge finish **one** opening edge, keeping other edge free. Tie off thread chains and tuck ends inside opening edges.

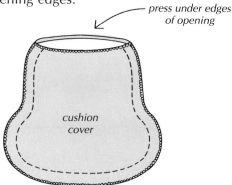

— press under edges of opening

cushion cover

4. Pop in pillow or several layers of thick batting shaped to fill the cover. Hand sew opening closed. Machine stitch ½" from edge across back of cover, using a zipper foot if necessary. This is a little tricky, but it can be done!

5. Machine or hand tack large, double-layer fabric strips finished with rolled edges to back corners and tie cushions to chair.

9. Terrific Tassels

Using serger chain made at the rolled-edge setting (page 148), you can make beautiful tassels in a matter of minutes for as little as $1 each, depending on the cost of the threads you combine. Use tassels to add panache to drapery tiebacks and pillows, to finish the ends of bolsters and table runners, or to enhance the keys to an armoire or jewelry box. Embellish Christmas stockings (page 113), or decorate an entire Christmas tree or wreath with tassels and fabric bows!

We made the richly-colored tassels by stacking a spool of black/multicolored Candlelight metallic thread on top of a spool of red Decor 6, then threading them as one through the upper looper. We stitched over one strand of #5 pearl cotton for added bulk.

To make tassels from serger chain:

1. Wrap serger chain around a piece of cardboard cut the desired length of tassel. Experiment. The more chain you wrap, the fuller and fatter the tassel. Tie a length of serger chain under tassel loops at one end of cardboard. Cut strands at other end. Seal with Fray Check or leave ends raw.

2. Tightly wrap another length of chain around tassel about ½" from top; knot securely. Seal ends with Fray Check. Tie or hand sew tassel in place.

10. Easy Chair-back Slipcover and Seat Makeover

This hardwood chair came with the dressing table but Barbara wasn't crazy about its looks and the upholstered seat was old and worn. We softened it with a padded chair-back slipcover and recovered the seat to match, adding a short ruffled skirt. It was a quick and easy way to give an old chair new life with just a little sewing—and stapling!

1. Unscrew seat. Remove old covering or cover over it, centering any obvious print pattern on the seat. For more cushioning, staple layers of polyester fleece to seat, then wrap and stretch fabric over it, pulling it smooth and taut. Staple it to underside of seat frame.

2. Cut ruffle desired width plus ½" seam allowance and 2½ to 3 times length around chair seat. Narrowly hem two short ends. Roll-edge finish one long edge; easestitch remaining edge and draw up to fit around seat. Staple in place. Cover all raw edges with firmly woven poplin "liner" stapled in place. Replace chair seat.

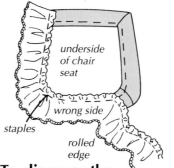

underside of chair seat

wrong side

staples

rolled edge

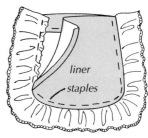

liner

staples

To slipcover the chair back:

1. Make a test pattern. Trace around back onto muslin or tissue. Add 2" all around. Cut two layers.

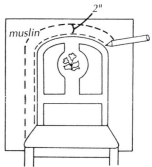

muslin

2"

2. Pin fit muslin test pattern on chair back. Remove and trim away excess pattern beyond pins, leaving a ½" seam allowance at outer edge and a 1" hem allowance at bottom edge. Unpin.

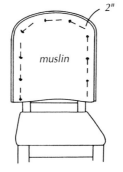

muslin
2"

3. Cut two chair backs from fabric and pad with polyester fleece, trimming away fleece hem allowance. Finish bottom edges with 3-thread balanced serger stitch.

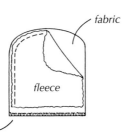

fabric
fleece
serging

4. Cut two ruffle strips 2" wide and 2½ to 3 times the distance around outer edge of pattern. **Wrong sides together**, roll-edge finish one long edge, curving at ends. Easestitch ½" and ¼" from raw edge.

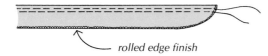

rolled edge finish

5. Pin ruffle to a chair-back cover, placing ends 1" from bottom edge. Adjust gathers to fit. Pin and stitch to remaining cover. Stitch close to first stitching and trim close to second stitching. Turn right side out. Press up and stitch 1"-deep hem.

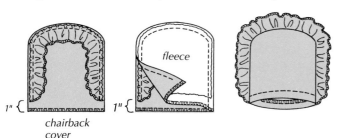

1"   1"
chairback
cover
fleece

11. Antique Dressing Screen

We layered two prints in the panels of this reversible antique Victorian dressing screen. One edge of a coordinating print band was roll-edge finished, then edgestitched to the top and bottom of each panel. Then the top and bottom edges of the panels were roll-edge finished.

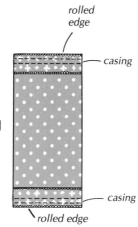

rolled edge
casing
casing
rolled edge

Finally the coordinating panels for each screen opening were edgestitched, wrong sides together, just below the rolled edge. A second row of stitching at both ends created the casing for the dowels.

Dressing screens look best when the panels are cut at least twice the width of the actual opening between the vertical bars. If possible use the selvage as the edge finish on the panels or finish with a rolled edge or narrow hem.

12. Pleated Trim for Drapery Tiebacks and Towels

We made picture-perfect pleats for decorative touches on drapery tiebacks and towels using the "Perfect Pleater," available by mail from Clotilde. (See page 155 for Resource List.) Tuck fabric into this special louvered strip of firm fabric and press to create evenly spaced pleats. A 45" length of fabric pleats down to approximately 14" of ¼"-wide knife-edge pleats. For longer ruffles, piece fabric strips first.

To make a pleated ruffle:

1. Roll-edge finish one long edge of ruffle strip.

2. Make ¼"-deep pleats following package directions. Begin by lining up rolled edge with one edge of pleater. Tuck fabric into first louver. Continue to end of pleater.

3. Press with steam iron and press cloth. Allow to cool and dry completely before removing. To help set pleats use a press cloth dampened in a solution of 1 part vinegar, 9 parts water.

> **NOTE:** Unless fabric has a high polyester content, pleats may not be permanent through laundering.

4. Machine baste ¼" from raw edge of pleated strip to secure pleats.

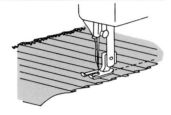

To make towel borders:

Wash towels 2 to 3 times **before** applying the trim to allow for shrinkage. It's a good idea to preshrink the fabric too.

1. Cut pleated fabric strip to fit across width of towel plus ½". Roll-edge to finish ends.

2. Roll-edge finish both long edges of a fabric strip 1" longer than towel width. Lap and edgestitch one edge of strip over raw edge of pleated fabric trim with ½" of band extending at each end.

3. Pin trim to towel, turn under ½" at each end and edgestitch all around band.

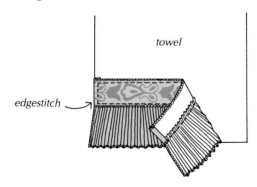

To make drapery tiebacks:

1. For each tieback cut two fabric strips the desired length plus ½". Roll-edge finish one long edge of each strip.

2. With wrong sides together, roll-edge finish remaining edges of the tieback.

3. Cut pleated trim to fit between tieback layers, plus ½". Roll-edge finish short ends.

4. Sandwich trim between tieback layers. Pin and edgestitch just inside rolled edge.

5. Whipstitch small plastic drapery rings to ends and hook onto cup hooks screwed into woodwork or wall.

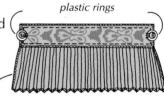

plastic rings

wrong side

13. Fabric-Covered File Boxes

Barbara's business filing system for her color clients resides in fabric-covered boxes that hide neatly under the daybed. Other similar boxes expand her out-of-season clothing storage space. The dressing table drawers hide all her tools, props and makeup.

We purchased inexpensive, knock-down cardboard file boxes at an office supply store and used transfer web (page 64) to bond the fabric to the boxes **before** assembling.

14. Candlestick Lamp

Can't find the perfect lamp? Do what Barbara did. Hunt down a pewter or silver (or brass) candlestick and have it drilled and wired for a lamp base. Add a cute shade and—VOILÀ—a one-of-a-kind desk or dressing table lamp!

The Ultrasuede Library

This library in Linda's home is an inviting cocoon with walls upholstered in Ultrasuede Facile. The transformation is wonderful! What we wanted was a rich mix of color, pattern and texture. We knew we wanted the Ultrasuede, but what color? There were so many from which to choose. (Fabric stores will often special order colors not in their stock.)

Linda had the shelves built when she and Bill moved into the house, then painted them dark green while the plan for the rest of the room was still a fuzzy vision. The rug came next, and then the Scheherazade paisley from Creative Home Textiles that we used in the slipcovers and Roman shades for the windows. Then it was clear that Dessert Rose was the perfect color for the walls. The wallpaper above the picture rail was the ideal coordinating element to finish the rich and cozy room.

1. *The Wall—Upholstered with Ultrasuede Facile using Quik Trak and Hobbs batting. Wallpaper above picture rail is "Chinon Ports of Call" from Katzenback and Warren.*
2. *Assorted SIMPLE "art" pillows made from Ultrasuede and Facile with serged details using interesting, unlabeled threads found in a yarn shop.*
3. *Facile lap quilt filled with Hobbs batting.*
4. *Insulated Roman shades from Creative Home Textile's Scheherazade (Torrence Place Collection), filled with Warm Windows batting.*
5. *Traditional slipcovers of the same fabric.*
6. *FAST, EASY sponge-painted "recycled" lamp and fireplace facade.*

The print over the fireplace is by Libby Unthank, the other by Kathy Kifer. The candlesticks are by sculptor Eric Canon.

127

1. The Walls

The Facile-upholstered walls were done with Quik Trak using the same techniques as on pages 28-29. With all the bookshelves, there really wasn't a lot of wall space so the project wasn't too cost-prohibitive—especially since we found the perfect wallpaper to use above the picture rail.

> **NOTE:** We mounted the Facile **horizontally** above the computer area and fireplace because the depth of the area to be covered was less than the width of the fabric, which meant less waste. AND it was faster!

2. The Ultrasuede Pillows

To continue the Ultrasuede theme Linda designed these wonderful, creative pillows:

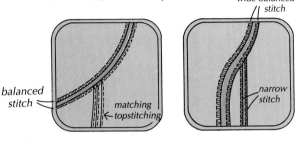

balanced stitch / matching topstitching / wide balanced stitch / narrow stitch

balanced stitch / Facile / glue down or fuse / print / blanket stitch

NOTE: *The facile insert is a rectangle gathered to fit.*

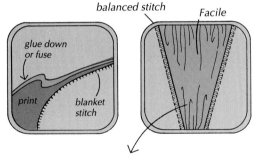

zigzag over cord

├3"┤ ├─15"─┤ ├3"┤

15" / Facile / 15"

├─5½"─┤ ├─5½"─┤

Ultrasuede / ├─9"─┤ / Ultrasuede

Topstitch Ultrasuede to Facile / stitch over gathers to secure / 15"

├─5½"─┼─4"─┼─5½"─┤
├────15"────┤

Once the fronts are completed, construct these simple pillows. (For inserting a zipper in back, see pg. 35.)

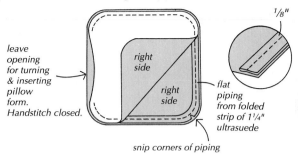

leave opening for turning & inserting pillow form. Handstitch closed. / right side / right side / ⅛" / flat piping from folded strip of 1¼" ultrasuede

snip corners of piping

3. The Lap Quilt

More Facile! This time in a lap-size quilt to snuggle under while reading in front of the fire on a blustery winter night. This is Linda's design:

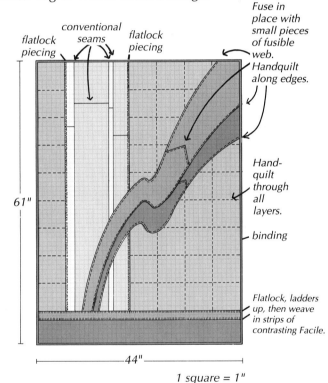

flatlock piecing / conventional seams / flatlock piecing / Fuse in place with small pieces of fusible web. Handquilt along edges. / 61" / Hand-quilt through all layers. / binding / Flatlock, ladders up, then weave in strips of contrasting Facile. / ├────44"────┤

1 square = 1"

> **NOTE:** Observe the piecing on the curved area and in the vertical bars. Also note quilt width. These widths were determined by the fabric width. To avoid buying lots of yardage to get a long, narrow strip, Linda made sure that no individual "accent color" piece was more than 44" long—the **width** of the fabric. Some are shorter, just for interest.

Following the grid above, draw the pattern onto a large piece of paper. (Linda used a roll of newsprint purchased from the local newspaper.) Transfer all markings. Then cut pattern apart to create individual patterns for each fabric piece. **Remember to add seam allowances to the straight-sided pieces.** Facile is soft, and unlike Ultrasuede, is easier to sew with conventional seams. The sides of the curved pieces don't need seam allowances since they are topstitched in place, then hand-quilted along the cut edges to avoid the challenge of seaming curves.

The back is one solid piece except for the border across the bottom. Quilting the layers creates a "pattern" on the reverse side of the completed quilt.

flatlocking

Hand-Quilting

paisley

Hand-quilting is easiest with a quilting frame. If you do not have one, use a table large enough to support the entire quilt.

1. Sandwich batting between top and bottom layers. If you are not working on a quilting frame, smooth and pin together every 6" (page 37).

2. Transfer quilting pattern to quilt top with erasable marker. Hand quilt through all layers using waxed quilting thread and working from the center out.

3. Trim away any uneven edges after quilting.

4. Cut a 2"-wide strip of Facile 6 yards long to bind the edges, piecing as necessary. Stitch to quilt front, **right sides together**. Wrap to back, turn under ½" and pin in place. Settle into that wing chair in front of the fire (or TV!) in YOUR library to handstitch the binding to the back of the quilt.

4. Insulated Roman Shades

These blinds are very similar to the ones in Bill and Linda's bedroom, page 30, but they are insulated with a layer of Warm Winter batting to keep the room even cozier. The other differences:

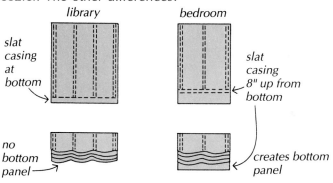

library

slat casing at bottom

no bottom panel

bedroom

slat casing 8" up from bottom

creates bottom panel

5. Slipcovers

When Linda's search for a set of wing chairs ended to no avail, we decided to transform these chairs with custom-made slipcovers. Now they're a "matched pair." We relied on a slipcover pro. If you'd rather do them yourself, see the Resource List (page 155).

6. Sponge Painting

No, this isn't sewing. But it **is** QUICK decorating. The lamp, a $3 thrift shop find, was a horrid mud color. The fireplace was painted beige by previous owners. Someday it will be retiled in variegated slate; for now it wears a temporary cloak of sponge painting.

We had a quart of terra cotta latex paint the same color as the Facile. That was no accident—we cleverly purchased it in the color we thought we wanted for the Facile so we could test it on the wall **before** we committed to purchasing the Facile! The green latex was left from similar testing before purchasing the oil-based enamel for the bookshelves and woodwork.

For the lamp:

1. Use masking tape to cover areas not to be painted.
2. Use a small piece of natural sea sponge to apply terra cotta paint to lamp base. Use a small brush to get into small areas if necessary. Let dry to the touch (30 minutes or so for latex paint).
3. Pour ½ cup of same color paint into a wide bowl. Stir in a squirt of red acrylic artist's paint. Sponge over lamp base until you get desired effect.

NOTE: Practice first. When painting the base color, paint a piece of paper to use as your practice "canvas."

For the fireplace: First paint a base coat of terra cotta, then sponge on the green with a **light touch**.

Accessory Ideas: The wall, quilt and pillow projects generated Ultrasuede scraps. Use them for desk accessories (wrap a can to hold pencils), picture hanging strips, a braided cord to tie around the lamp base, and a phone book or address book cover:

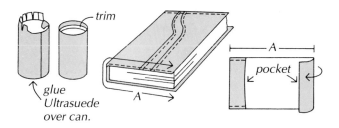

trim

glue Ultrasuede over can.

pocket

A

Pati Palmer's Sewing Room

Welcome to Pati's state-of-the-art sewing room designed by Lynette Ranney Black. Pati and her associates try out new sewing machines and sergers, test sewing techniques for the Palmer/Pletsch patterns licensed to McCall's, and film sewing videos in this well-organized space. We've included a floor plan.

Since light is so important in a sewing room, Pati opted for white walls and European cabinets (from a kitchen cabinet source). We enlivened the stark white space with bright splashes of color at the windows and with coordinating cushions (see mattress cover how-tos on page 134) and throw pillows in the window seats. Fabric storage tubes and a slipcovered folding screen complete the picture. We even recovered the chair seats.

When planning your sewing space, leave some wall space free for prints or posters, a bulletin board with inspiring magazine clips, and racks for threads and notions. Old type cases make great thread displayers. And every sewing room needs a VCR, so a special space was planned to house one here.

130

1. Window Treatment

Claessen's "Magic" hardware made it unbelievably easy to drape the windows with puffy swags.

1. Mount two tulip swag-holders at one corner of each window. Also mount a fat, painted wooden curtain rod across window.

2. To determine width and length of swags for window, buy several yards of muslin and experiment. It takes about 16" of extra fabric for a small pouf or 24" for a large one. Finish swags with decorative rolled edges all around.

3. With swag folded into loose pleats, loosely drape around curtain rod and pull about 8-10" of fabric (more for larger poufs) through the hardware; fluff to form pouf that hides hardware. Carefully tuck tissue paper inside folds of draped swag for a fuller, rounder look. Repeat with second swag.

2. Fabric Storage Tubes

Whenever possible, Pati likes to store special fabrics on tubes—and in a sono tube covered with fabric! Sono tubes are concrete forms you can buy from building construction suppliers. Available in diameters from 4"-48", they're usually sold by the foot,

diameters from 4"-48", they're usually sold by the foot, are inexpensive and make great storage containers as well as table bases, plant stands, and stools.

1. Cut fabric the height of tube, plus 6" and the tube circumference, plus 1". Finish top and bottom edges with balanced 3-thread serging.

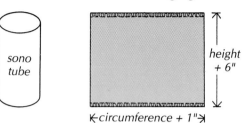

2. Seam ends together, turn right side out and slide fabric tube over sono tube. (It should fit snugly!) Turn serged ends to inside and glue in place with white fabric glue such as Sobo.

3. For trim, stitch contrasting piping to both long edges of a 3½"-wide strip of coordinating fabric cut to fit around tube and allowing 1" for overlap. Then decoratively serge over piping seam allowances with cord riding under presser foot. Use a contrasting color of Decor 6 in the upper looper and a balanced 3-thread stitch.

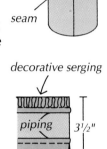

4. Glue trim to tube, turning under ½" where ends meet. Hold in place with push pins while drying.

3. Folding Screen

Use a folding screen to close off a dressing area or to create hidden storage space in an unused corner of your sewing room (a great place to hide your fabric stash!). If you borrow sewing space from another room in the house, a screen makes the perfect room divider. Pati's doubles as a bulletin board since it's simply three sheets of foam-center board (Foamcore) in an easy-to-make fabric "slipcover." Our inspiration was from the folding screen project in the Instant Interiors booklet, **Fabric Spacemakers**. (See page 156.)

Each panel in our tri-fold screen is 20" x 64". Yours can be any size appropriate for your purpose and space limitations. We suggest purchasing ¼"-thick Foamcore from your local frame shop. If you don't have a steady hand with yardstick and utility knife, ask the shop to cut the foam to the desired dimensions.

1. Cut two pieces of fabric (front and back) large enough to hold all three screen panels, allowing for ½" seam allowances on two long edges and top, ½" in each panel section for thickness of foam, and ¼" for each "hinge" between panels. Finish bottom edge of each piece with balanced 3-thread serging. If you must piece fabric, position piecing seams at "hinge" locations (step 3).

PRO TIP: When using printed fabric with an obvious direction (stripe, plaid, diagonal), make sure it's printed on grain.

DESIGNER TIP: Use coordinating prints on front and back of screen. Pati's has green and white stripes on the reverse side.

2. Stitch front to back, **right sides together**, along top and sides. Turn right side out. Smooth layers together and pin randomly to prevent shifting while stitching "hinges" for panel compartments.

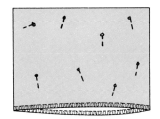

3. To create "hinges", mark stitching lines, measuring in from sides the foam panel width, **plus** ½". Starting at top of slipcover, machine stitch on each line and again ¼" away from first stitching toward the center of the panel. Slide foam board into pockets.

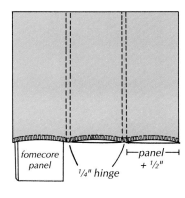

fomecore panel   ¼" hinge   panel + ½"

4. Chair Seat Covers

Many chairs have seats that pop out, making an instant transformation a breeze!

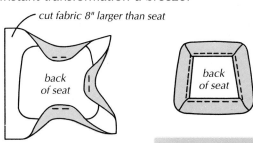

cut fabric 8" larger than seat

back of seat

back of seat

Staple, pulling fabric taut and alternating from side to side, folding corners in neatly.

NOTE: If chair needs more padding, cut 1 or more layers of batting to size and place between fabric and chair before stapling.

The Floor Plan

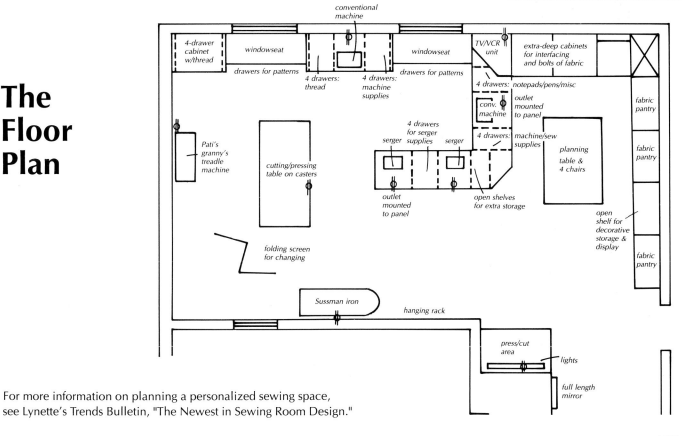

conventional machine

4-drawer cabinet w/thread

windowseat

drawers for patterns

windowseat

drawers for patterns

TV/VCR unit

extra-deep cabinets for interfacing and bolts of fabric

4 drawers: thread

4 drawers: machine supplies

4 drawers: notepads/pens/misc

outlet mounted to panel

conv. machine

fabric pantry

Pati's granny's treadle machine

cutting/pressing table on casters

4 drawers for serger supplies

serger   serger

4 drawers: machine/sew supplies

planning table & 4 chairs

fabric pantry

outlet mounted to panel

open shelves for extra storage

open shelf for decorative storage & display

fabric pantry

folding screen for changing

Sussman iron

hanging rack

press/cut area

lights

full length mirror

For more information on planning a personalized sewing space, see Lynette's Trends Bulletin, "The Newest in Sewing Room Design."

133

1. NO-SEW dinette cushions and mattress cover with fabric piping.
2. Lined curtains with rolled-edge finish.
3. Curtain tiebacks with rolled-edge chain trim.

Travel Trailer Facelift

A recreational vehicle is a fun place to use your home dec skills...and small, so costs can be lower. Let your alter ego show here, like Lynette did. She and her husband purchased a vintage 1964 trailer, then gave it a full facelift—new paint job, new floor, and dressed up with new curtains and cushion covers in colors Lynette loved that just didn't fit into her home.

1. Dinette and Bed Cushions

We recovered the existing cushions with a vibrantly dyed denim, an inexpensive yet durable fabric that's perfect for vacation living and tough treatment from rough and tumble campers. Cushion shapes and sizes in campers, boats and recreational vehicles vary, so it's a good idea to make a diagram as you take them apart.

> **NOTE:** The dye in denim can rub off on clothing and skin. Have it set by your dry cleaner. A cup of vinegar in the washer works too, but can leave the denim wrinkled and less crisp looking.

The existing dinette seat backs were made of 4"-thick foam glued to plywood. We gave them a "lift" by padding top and sides with quilt batting. Since denim stretches, we cut the new covers slightly smaller for a snug fit. We placed the newly assembled covers over the batting-padded cushions, pulled them taut and attached to the plywood backs with heavy-duty staples.

We replaced the well-worn bunk mattress with 4"-thick foam softened with a wrap of quilt batting. Mattress foam is often available from fabric stores specializing in home decorating, or check the Yellow Pages under "foam." Welting on the mattress cover adds a bright, decorative touch plus seam durability.

To cover the mattress:

1. Measure foam and cut top and bottom cover to fit; add ½" all around for seams. Cut boxing strip the width of mattress thickness plus 1", and long enough to fit around mattress.

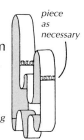

piece as necessary

boxing strip

2. Cut bias fabric strips wide enough to fit snugly around welting cord, plus 1", piecing as necessary to fit around both edges of boxing strip.

NOTE: Save yardage by cutting welting strips for straight edges on straight of grain. **It must be bias-cut for curves**.

3. Wrap fabric over cord, **wrong sides together**, and stitch next to cord using a zipper foot.

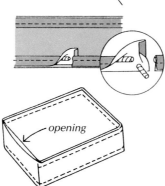

4. Stitch welting to both edges of boxing strip using zipper foot, overlapping ends as shown.

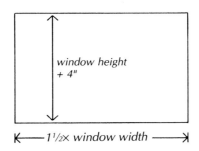

5. Pin and stitch boxing strip to cover top and bottom, leaving one short end open.

opening

6. Turn right sides out. Insert mattress and hand stitch opening closed.

2. Curtains

Boldly colored curtains add a splash of color and needed privacy. A lining protects them from an early death from sun fading and decay. We made them simple since we chose such a boldly colored fabric!

1. To determine curtain size, add a total of 4" to window height for hem and rod pocket and 1½ times the width.

window height + 4"

← 1½× window width →

2. Cut curtain to determined dimensions; cut lining ¼" shorter. Serge bottom edges of both. Press up 1"-wide hem on each and twin needle stitch from right side stitching close to serged edge.

curtain fabric

(hem lining separately)

3. Serge lining to curtain, **wrong sides together**, at top edge. Roll-edge finish sides, treating the two fabrics as one. Lining will be ¼" shorter than curtain.

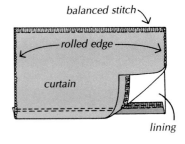

balanced stitch
rolled edge
curtain
lining

4. Press under 2" at top for rod pocket and twin needle stitch as for bottom hem.

3. Curtain Tiebacks

We created these decorative curtain tiebacks with rolled-edge chain embellishment (page 148).

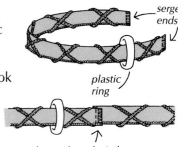

1. Wrap a 1½"x15" fabric strip around 5/32" cording. **Guide encased cording under serger presser foot** and finish with decorative rolled edge, stitching as close to cording as possible.

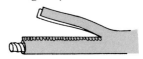

2. Using two strands of contrasting decorative rolled-edge chain (page 148), criss-cross cording, securing at each cross and chain ends with a dot of white fabric glue.

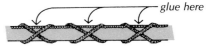

glue here

3. Serge cording ends. Slide a small plastic drapery ring over cord. Lap ends and machine stitch. Hook in place over cup hook screwed into wall.

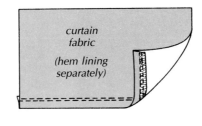

serge ends
plastic ring
lap ends and stitch

Even the towels are handmade! We cut toweling fabric to size and finished with rolled edges using standard serging thread.

The Veranda

Can't you just imagine a leisurely al fresco lunch on Pati's veranda? Lunch is served on pink "Spackleware" hand-made Italian dinnerware from Mamma Ro', with refreshing lemonade filling the Mamma Ro' handblown glassware. Cool, cotton prints from Fabric Traditions mix and match in table coverings and the comfy throw pillows and cushions in the wicker chairs, copies of 1908 originals. (Coincidentally, that's the year the house was completed!)

The conversation grouping provides a comfortable place away from the table to relax with coffee and Linda's decadent brownies, while the gentle greyhound "house guest" (with an award-winning past as a racer) looks on.

1. *EASY table top cloths with rolled edges in pearl cotton.*
2. *Undercloth with flatlocking in pearl cotton.*
3. *QUICK Double-sided napkins with rolled edges pearl cotton.*
4. *Chair cushions with balanced stitch in pearl cotton.*
5. *EASY throw pillows with serger ties.*
6. *Ribbon streamers finished with rolled edges.*

1. Table Top Cloths

We topped the table with two square cloths, one placed diagonally over the other so all corners show against the undercloth. Self-knots at the corners of the larger floral cloth and silver bells tied to the corners of the smaller one on top add weight to keep the cloths in place on breezy days.

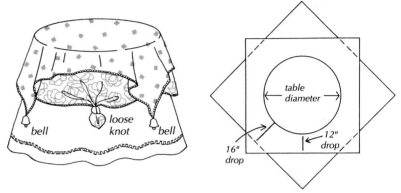

bell   loose knot   bell

table diameter

16" drop

12" drop

Cut each cloth to desired size. Roll-edge finish, leaving long serger tails at corners of smaller cloth to tie on the bells.

2. Underscloth

1. Cut a to-the-floor cloth (page 13), adding 3½" all around for the padded hem.

2. Cut a 3¼"-wide strip of batting and machine baste to **wrong side** around edge of cloth. Butt edges of batting together where piecing is necessary.

3. Serge a flatlocked hem with loops on outside and pearl cotton in upper looper:

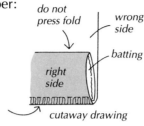

*Turn 3½"-wide hem to **wrong side** over batting, then turn again.*

Press lightly along edge.

Flatlock next to fold, being careful not to cut fold.

Pull hem down until stitching is flat.

WARNING TIP: ONE layer of batting is enough. We originally wanted a really puffy bottom edge—but the whole thing stuck out like a crinoline skirt!

3. Napkins

These are our usual quick-serge napkins—double-sided squares of complementary fabrics **wrong sides together** with rolled edges.

4. Chair Cushions

The serging here is both utilitarian and decorative. A balanced stitch sets off the padded flange around the seat-back cushions. We made traditional box cushions for the seats. (See mattress cover how-tos, page 134.) Both cushions are finished with custom-made piping at the outer edges.

1. Cut cushion backs from geometric print, using pattern you created. Cut cushion fronts from floral print, making them 2½" smaller on sides and top as shown. From a third coordinating print, cut a 4"-wide flange strip for each cushion with a length equal to side and top edges of the cushion back (A).

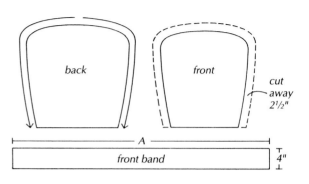

2. Zigzag over a cord placed next to seamline on one long edge of each flange.

3. Pin flange to cushion front, **right sides together**, pulling on cord to gather slightly at corners to fit. Stitch. Remove cord.

4. Press seam open, then fold band against cushion front, **wrong sides together**. Flatlock with stitches hanging over folded edge, with pearl cotton in upper looper. Be careful not to cut fabric. Open out flange so flatlocking lies flat.

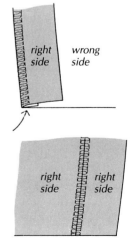

5. Make enough piping from flange fabric to fit around outer edges of each cushion back (A) and both edges of boxing strip for each seat cushion.

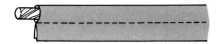

6. Machine baste piping to cushion back. Stitch, back to front, **right sides together**, using zipper foot to get close to piping. Leave bottom edge open. Turn and press.

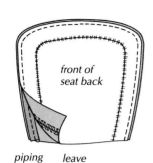

front of seat back

piping   *leave bottom open*

7. Topstitch along inside edge of flatlocking through all layers to create flange, stopping ½" from bottom edge.

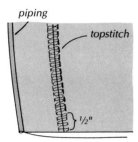

piping

topstitch

½"

8. Stuff flange with polyester fiberfill until firm. Fill cushion with polyester fiberfill to desired thickness and firmness.

> **QUICK TIP:** Use the handle of a wooden spoon to coax filling into place in flange.

9. Turn in raw edges at bottom of cushion and whipstitch folded edges together.

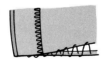

5. Throw Pillows

For the veranda we made both Turkish and reverse Turkish throw pillows, alternating fabric prints. We used 16" pillow forms from Hobbs.

1. Cut 17" squares for pillow fronts. (If making reverse Turkish corners, see step 1 at right.)

2. Cut two rectangles for each back, each 17" x 9", and insert zippers down center (page 35). **Unzip zipper.**

3. Stitch front to back, **right sides together**.

For Turkish corners (rounded, gathered corners):

1. Mark corners as shown.

2. Zigzag over cord on diagonal lines. Draw up cord to gather corners.

3. Stitch several rows just inside of gathering to secure corners.

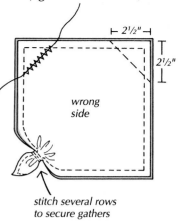

2½"

2½"

wrong side

stitch several rows to secure gathers

4. Turn cover right side out and insert pillow form.

For reverse Turkish corners
(with bow-tied "ears"):

1. When cutting out pillows cut pillow corners as shown, creating "ears"

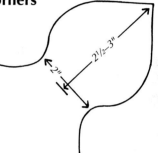

2½-3"

2"

3. After turning pillows right sides out, gather and tie corners with serger rolled-edge chain (page 148).

4. Insert pillow form and zip closed.

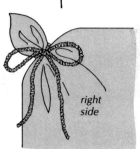

right side

6. Ribbon Banner

Interior designer Virginia Burney created this delightful ribbon banner with a combination of purchased ribbon and serger ribbon (fabric strips finished with decorative rolled edges). The ribbons are tied to a large key ring snapped to a fishing swivel mounted on the top of a bamboo pole, leaving the ribbon free to flutter in the breeze.

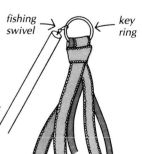

fishing swivel   *key ring*

1. *QUICK AND EASY runner with Woolly Nylon rolled edges and napkins with pearl cotton rolled edge.*

2. *SIMPLE box cushions with Woolly Nylon rolled-edge seams*

3. *EASY pillow.*

4. *Creative kites and banners.*

A Terrace Buffet

Linda and Bill find it hard to resist their colorful backyard terrace and garden all summer long. It beckons invitingly with a changing panorama of aromatic herbs, tasty home-grown vegetables and glorious flowers (many of them edible), all planted expressly for Linda's colorful culinary creations.

In keeping with the bright garden atmosphere, we chose a cheery print from P. Kaufmann for cushions and table runners, and rejuvenated the furniture with a fresh coat of deep blue paint to match. Then we pulled out Bill's boyhood toy truck and Deborah Carnes' antique Bauerware dishes, filled the wheelbarrow with ice-cold drinks—and had a watermelon party to celebrate a job well done!

1. Runner and Napkins

The runner is simply a rectangle of fabric serged with a rolled edge using Woolly Nylon—a tough, sturdy thread to use on outdoor projects (as long as you don't use a hot iron on it!). When placed straight on the table, about 5" of table shows on each side. The drop at each end is 14". However, when we set the table for our watermelon party, putting it on an angle was livelier and much more interesting!

> **DESIGNER TIP:** Think about angling cloths, rugs, even furniture when arranging a room or a table. Sometimes having everything lined up parallel is static, lacking energy. Putting something askew can add spark to a room!

The napkins reverse the color scheme—bright yellow, textured shirting fabric finished with a rolled edge using blue pearl cotton.

2. Outdoor Furniture Cushions

The chaise lounge and two chairs came with their own cushions. We ordered 3"-thick foam cushions, custom-cut at a foam supply house, to fit the remaining chairs, then made removable covers for all. To make removable box cushion covers, follow the mattress cover directions on page 134, adding a zipper in one side panel like we did in the window seat cushions for the playroom, page 66.

In place of piping at the edges, we simply serge-seamed the boxing strips to the cushion covers (top and bottom) with **wrong sides together**, using a rolled edge stitch and yellow Woolly Nylon thread in the upper looper.

> **A word about outdoor furniture fabric selection:** When selecting fabric for outdoor use remember that darker and brighter colors tend to fade more quickly, *especially* red.
>
> **And a word about care:** Any fabric, including plastic, will suffer if left out in sun or rain too long. Find a good storage place for your cushions when you are not using them. For added protection, use Scotchguard or other waterproofing spray, and reapply on a regular basis.

3. Pillows

We purchased this knife-edge striped pillow, but it would be **very** easy to make from a favorite fabric. Create your own custom-striped fabric—serge together different colored strips of fabric or ribbon.

4. Creative Kites and Banners

No, we didn't make the cheerful dragonfly. But, we could have, using sturdy, weatherproof nylon thread and fabrics available in stores that carry outerwear fabrics and using serger piecing (page 92) and applique techniques (page 44). Here are a few other design ideas:

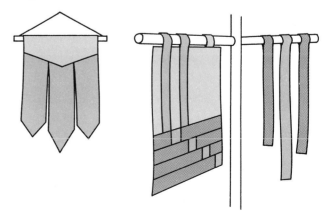

This is our fourth serger book, so this special section includes only basic information to help you with the decorating projects described here. We highly recommend these books for reference and more creative serging ideas: **Sewing with Sergers, Creative Serging,** and **The Serger Idea Book**. (See page 159.)

Serger Stitch Types

The five basic serger stitches suggested for decorating projects are:

3-thread overlock: 3 threads connect or "lock" at the seamline and the stitch appearance is similar on both sides. This stitch is most often used for balanced, decorative stitching.

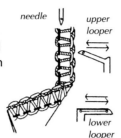

3/4-thread overlock: Has the appearance of a 3-thread stitch with an extra needle thread running down the middle. On most machines, you can remove the right needle for a wide 3-thread stitch or the left needle for a narrower 3-thread stitch.

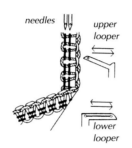

3/4-thread overlock variation: Looks different from the above stitch. The lower looper thread is caught by **both** needles and the upper looper by only the right needle, leaving a row of what looks like straight stitching next to the serging. This means you **must** use both needles if you want a wide stitch. However, you can leave out the left needle for a narrower stitch.

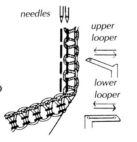

2-thread overedge: Called an "overedge" because the threads do not connect or "lock" at the seamline. It is not used to sew seams. It can be used as an edge finish and is perfect for flatlocking.

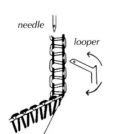

5-thread stitch: Consists of a 2-thread chain stitch and a 3-thread overlock stitch creating a strong seam.

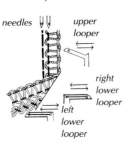

Stitch Width

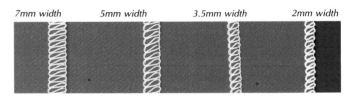

7mm width   5mm width   3.5mm width   2mm width

On some sergers, you adjust stitch width by turning a dial that moves the stitch finger and knives (infinite widths available). On others, you change the needle position to the right or left needle hole.

Some machines have a 7.5mm stitch width capability with a 3-thread stitch, others a 5mm maximum and some just a 3.5mm maximum width. For the most decorative potential, we suggest sergers with **at least** a 5mm width.

Stitch Length

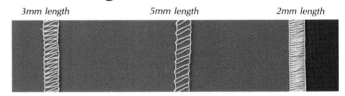

3mm length   5mm length   2mm length

Adjust stitch length by turning a dial that changes the amount of fabric the feed dogs move. Most machines can sew a very short stitch length (0.5mm) up to a long stitch length (4-5mm). Often a **slight** change in stitch length will improve stitch appearance.

Tension Tips

Mastering tension adjustment is the key to enjoying your serger's versatility. Think of tension dials as "pattern adjusters." For flatlocking, rolled edges or using decorative threads, you must know how to adjust the tensions. We'll use a 3-thread stitch as our example in the following illustrations.

The perfect balanced stitch is one in which the upper and lower looper threads meet at and hang slightly over the edge of the fabric. The width of the loops on the top is the same as on the bottom.

142

Unbalanced 3-thread tension:
The upper looper thread is pulled to the underside. To balance, loosen the thread that is too tight **first**. Loosen lower looper until it comes out to the edge. Test, then tighten upper looper if necessary.

Unbalanced 3-thread tension:
The lower looper thread is pulled to the top. Loosen the upper looper until it comes out to the edge. Test, then tighten the lower looper if necessary.

Now check the needle thread.
If needle thread forms loops on underside, tighten needle thread tension. (With decorative thread, this may be caused by a too-tight lower looper thread.)

If you pull on the seam and you can see the needle thread, tighten needle tension for a stronger seam.

If the seam puckers, it usually indicates that the needle tension is too tight.

Heavier threads and yarns or ribbons require different tension than those for regular serger thread. They create more resistance in the tension dials because they take up more room. They require looser tension.

If your heavy thread is in the upper looper and you have loosened that dial as much as possible only to find the tension is still too tight, try tightening the lower looper to counteract the problem.

If tension is still a problem, remove upper looper thread from one or more thread guides, as long as it doesn't adversely affect feeding. As a last resort, remove thread from the upper looper tension disk. **Experiment!**

QUICK TIP: If your machine has inset dials, put a piece of Scotch Brand Magic Transparent Tape over the dial to keep the thread from falling into it.

Stitch Width and Length Affect Tension

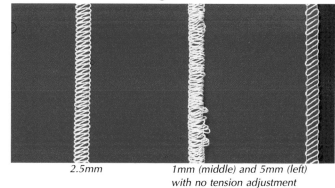

2.5mm   1mm (middle) and 5mm (left)
                         with no tension adjustment

If you change from a very wide stitch to a narrow one, less thread is required to form the loops; you will usually need to tighten the looper tensions. If you change from a narrow to a wide stitch, loosen the tensions to let more thread out of the disks to cover the wider width.

If you **increase** stitch length significantly, the looper threads will tighten up against the edge, causing thread "pokeys;" sometimes the fabric edge rolls into a "tunnel." More thread is needed to travel the longer distance from stitch to stitch. To correct, loosen tensions of **both** loopers, letting more thread through, until loops meet at and hang slightly over the edge, creating a balanced stitch.

If you **decrease** stitch length significantly, the stitch will look sloppy because there is simply too much thread. Less thread is needed for shorter stitch lengths. To correct, tighten the looper tensions, letting less thread through. Sometimes a slightly different stitch length improves the look of the stitch, too.

Fabric Thickness Affects Tension

Bulky fabrics require more thread to be released since the distance over and around the top and bottom layers has increased. If you don't loosen the tensions, the loopers will hug the edge too tightly, and may even cause tunneling at the edge and the "pokeys." **Thinner fabrics** may require tighter than average tensions; otherwise stitches may be too loopy and look sloppy.

NOTE: For an in-depth explanation of serger tension, see **Creative Serging** by Pati Palmer, Gail Brown and Sue Green and **The Serger Idea Book**, published by Palmer/Pletsch (page 159).

Securing Serged Seams

Securing the ends of serged seams is extremely important in home dec serging. This is especially true if the item will be washed frequently. Here are our favorite tricks for securing the chain.

Knotting Next to the Fabric

1. Tie a knot loosely. Slip a straight pin into its center.

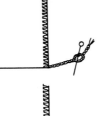

2. Wiggle knot over pin until it gets close to fabric edge.

3. With pin at fabric edge, slip knot to point. Pull tightly.

4. Dab with seam sealant such as Fray Check. After it dries, cut off the excess chain.

Burying the Chain

Thread tail chain through a large, blunt tapestry needle or loop turner. Pull chain under looper threads and cut off excess. Dab with Fray Check for durability.

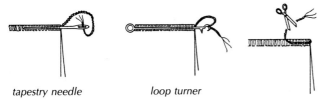

tapestry needle   *loop turner*

Turning Outside Corners

Napkins, placemats, valances, drapery panels, ruffles—you name it. Most home dec items have outside corners that need finishing. Use either method here.

The easiest way to turn an outside corner is to stitch off the edge at each corner, then pivot the fabric and stitch over stitching at previous corner. Tie off the tail at the last corner and apply seam sealant to the knot and to the other three corners.

To actually **turn** corners while serging:

1. Trim the adjacent edge along cutting line for 2" before serging to the corner. (Ignore this step if you don't have any seam or hem allowances to trim.)

2. Serge to one corner and off the edge **one stitch**. Raise the needle. (You can't pivot with the needle in fabric on a serger.) Raise the presser foot.

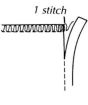
1 stitch

3. Pull a little slack in the needle thread so you can gently remove the chain (and the attached fabric) from the stitch finger. **Be careful**. Pulling too much slack will create a loop. If you accidentally pull too much, pull the excess up, just above the tension dial.

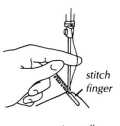
stitch finger

4. Pivot the fabric. Lower the needle into the fabric in the middle of the first serging and the same distance from the edge as the width of the serging. Continue serging to next corner and repeat these steps. Tie off or bury tail chain at last corner.

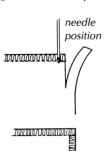
needle position

Turning Inside Corners

Some sewers think inside corners are easier to serge than outside corners.

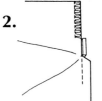
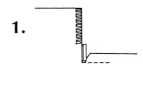
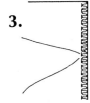

1.   **2.**   **3.**

1. Serge until the knife touches the corner. Stop with needle in fabric.

2. Straighten the corner **without** lifting the presser foot. You will see a "v"-shaped fold of fabric. Don't worry; you won't catch it in the serging!

3. Finish serging the straightened edge.

4. The finished inside corner will appear a bit rounded.

PRO TIP: If inside corner has a seam allowance to trim, mark cutting line within 1" of both sides of corner using an erasable marker. Clip to corner. Serge as above, trimming away seam allowance.

Serging in a Circle

This trick comes in handy for home dec serging on things like oval placemats and circular hem edges.

1. Pull out 2"-4"of unchained threads by creating slack in the needle thread between the needle and tension guide. Pull on chain to separate the threads. Rock the handwheel back and forth as you pull gently.

2. Begin in the middle of a long edge, not on a curve. Serge around the edge, just skimming it with the knives. Stop when you reach the beginning stitch.

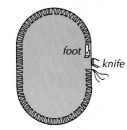

foot *knife*

3. Raise the upper knife. Serge two stitches over beginning stitches.

4. Again, pull out unchained threads (Step 1, above).

5. Tie a knot in each tail (less bulky than tieing a single knot in the chain). Dab knots with seam sealant. Cut off excess.

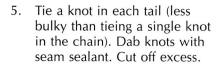

Also see **PRO TIP**, page 16.

Decorative Threads

Decorative threads make serging fun! There are an amazing number of threads, yarns, and ribbons that can be used for decorative serging. The following are the most readily available, **and** keep your eyes open for other possibilities. Yarn stores are a great source.

Decorative threads do affect your tension. (See tension on page 143). Also remember that not all machines can handle all decorative threads. Have patience, but also have an alternative in mind in case your first choice won't work.

Listed and described below are the decorative threads used for projects in this book:

Regular Thread—Available in several weights, from extra-fine to all-purpose. It is used mostly for seams, as an edge finish and for rolled hems.

Clear Nylon Monofilament Thread—We generally limit use of this thread to decorative applications where we want one or more of the threads to be invisible, as in flatlock fagotting.

Topstitching Thread—This thread is tightly twisted and a little heavier than regular thread so shows more at the finished edge. You can use it in the needle and both loopers. Use a spool cap so thread flows freely.

Rayon Thread—A number of decorative threads are made of rayon, so when we refer to fine rayon thread, we mean fine rayon machine embroidery thread. It has a beautiful sheen. Familiar brands include Madeira and Sulky.

Decor 6 is a medium-weight, untwisted rayon cord available to stores and consumers through Palmer/Pletsch. This thread makes a bolder statement as it fills in better and has exceptional luster due to its lack of twist. However, it is also more fragile than twisted thread. Therefore, we suggest it for items that will receive little wear and washing, window valances and holiday items, for example. Decor 6 can be used in the needle or in the loopers, but in no more than two places at once.

Texturized Nylon—Also called "woolly nylon," this fuzzy, stretchy thread can be used in the needle and both loopers. It is soft, extra strong, and available in a wide color range. Use a press cloth over it; a hot iron will melt it. Direct sunlight may cause yellowing. You will **always** need to loosen tension settings with this thread.

Metallic Thread—There are many wonderful metallic threads available in varying weights, stiffness and sheen. We recommend them in **loopers only**, as many of them fray in the needle.

Crochet Thread—This is a very durable, tightly twisted cord, slightly thicker than topstitching thread and available in cotton or fuzzier, more wool-like acrylic. Use in upper looper only.

Pearl Cotton—This all-cotton cord, similar to crochet thread, has a looser twist and a soft sheen. Two weights are appropriate for serger sewing: Finer #8 can be used in one or both loopers; thicker #5 can be used in only the upper looper.

Ribbon—Soft, **rayon** knitting ribbon, 1/16" to 1/8" wide, is appropriate for serging. This ribbon is also called ribbon floss. When used in the upper looper, ribbon creates an unusual, braid-like edge. Due to the thickness of ribbon floss, it can be used in only one looper at a time and not in the needle. **Do not** even attempt to use nylon or polyester ribbons; they're too stiff!

Yarn—Limit choices to machine knitting yarns and use only in the upper looper. Check the weight by running two strands through the looper eye. If you can't force a double strand through, then you can assume that one strand will not feed easily enough to work successfully.

How Much to Buy

As a rule, allow approximately seven yards of thread per looper for every one yard of decorative serging. In other words, if the special thread will be in both loopers, plan on 14 yards per yard of serging—more for very fine threads. Add about 10 yards for testing.

Decorative Thread Tips

- **Use decorative thread where it will show.** The upper looper thread shows on the finished edge. Not all machines work with decorative thread in two loopers.

- **Make threading easier.** Use the looper threader that came with your machine or try a dental floss threader, available at most drug stores.

- **"Clear" threads before beginning to stitch.** Bring all threads up. Use a pin to pull up needle thread to prevent it from looping around loopers. Then pull all threads under presser foot to hold threads in place while you form a chain.

use a pin to clear   *pull up needle thread*   *put all threads under presser foot*

Rotate the handwheel by hand to see if the stitches are forming a chain on the stitch finger.

- **Keep the thread chain under the "bridge"** at the back of the presser foot as you begin to serge.

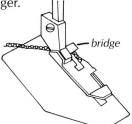

bridge

- **Be sure threads are engaged in tension discs** by tugging on them just above and below the dials. You should feel resistance on each thread.

- **Use spool caps** for parallel-wound spools and always place the spool's thread notch on the bottom, next to the thread platform.

spool cap

notch

- **Use thread nets over slippery and rough threads** (rayon, nylon and many metallics) to prevent spilling or slipping off the bottom of the spool. Fold net back on itself to allow the thread to flow smoothly without resistance.

fold net back

- **Hiccups** happen anytime there is a restriction on your thread—as if you suddenly increased the tension. You'll see them when the thread catches on something, such as the notch on a spool, or doesn't reel smoothly off the spool, ball or chain. Check.

To fix hiccups:

1. Rip out stitch to just above the hiccup.

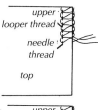

upper looper thread
needle thread
top

2. Unchain the tail chain (step 1, page 145). Lower needle into seamline a few stitches **above** where you stopped ripping as shown. Complete stitching.

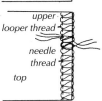

upper looper thread
needle thread
top

3. Go back to hiccup area and pull all threads to wrong side. Knot. Dab knots with seam sealant (Fray Check). Trim or bury threads in seam.

- **Start with a loose "pool" of thread** if thread, yarn or ribbon is not wound on spools or cones. This allows thread to feed freely. Place the ball or skein on the table behind the machine, then reel off a large quantity and alternately serge and reel, serge and reel.

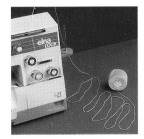

Or rewind thread onto an empty (or full) cone or spool. If winding by hand, "cross-wind" by moving the spool back and forth as you wind. This is great TV work!

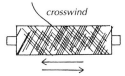

crosswind

- **Lift the presser foot and position fabric before serging** to prevent stitches from stacking up under the foot when you begin. You may also need to tug gently on the chain when beginning to serge.

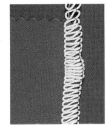

- **Begin serging slowly!** Although your serger was made for speed, heavier threads pose a variety of potential problems. In addition, serging too fast can place extra tension on the thread resulting in uneven stitching. Check your stitches every few inches.

- **ALWAYS TEST FIRST!!!** It is difficult and time-consuming to correct a mistake, so testing is essential to successful serging. Always test the thread of your choice on the fabric of your choice!

Flatlocking

The two-thread flatlock is the simplest to achieve. Sew the seam, pull it open and flatten.

Sew the seam.   *Pull it open.*

Many home sewers have 3- and 3/4-thread sergers, so Palmer/Pletsch Associates and other experts created a way to alter tensions so you can do flatlocking on them.

Flatlocking on 3- and 3/4-Thread Sergers

1. Loosen needle tension nearly all the way until thread forms a "V" on underside. Tighten lower looper nearly all the way until thread almost disappears, forming a nearly straight line at the edge. If the stitch doesn't look like this before you flatten the fabric, you don't have flatlocking!

2. Gently tug seam open to flatten. If flattened seam buckles under the upper looper stitches, it isn't flat enough. Loosen the tensions until seam lies flat.

3. On the top side you should see the loops of the upper looper. You should barely see a straight line on the right edge. That is the lower looper thread. On the underside, you should see a "ladder" formed by the needle thread.

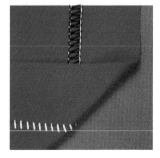

PRO TIP: It is sometimes difficult to get the lower looper tight enough for 3-thread flatlocking. Try one of the following:

· Use texturized nylon thread in the lower looper. It affects the tension the same as tightening the tension dial 2 or 3 numbers.

· Wrap the thread around the lower looper tension dial **twice**. Loosen the tension, then **gradually** tighten while serging **slowly** so you don't risk bending the lower looper.

· Some sergers have an **extra** lower looper tension disk for rolled-edge finishing. It can be used to tighten tension for flatlocking as well.

Use the widest stitch when flatlocking. It will be easier to flatten and more attractive. Stitch length is a matter of personal preference. Set it short if you want a solid band of color.

Flatlocking is reversible.

When you want loops on the right side, start with fabric **wrong sides together** and decorative thread in the upper looper.

For a "ladder" of stitches on the right side, start with fabric **right sides together**. Remember, if you want a decorative thread for the ladder, it must fit through the **needle**.

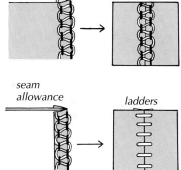

Flatlock Variations

Flatlock Faggoting: Create this delicate, hand-crafted look on light- or medium-weight fabric. See page 12 for how-to details.

Flatlock woven with ribbon: See pages 100-101.

Flatlock Couching: This is a method of applying cord or yarn to the surface of a fabric. (See page 83.) Use clear nylon thread in the needle, regular thread in the loopers. Tuck yarn into a fold. Flatlock on the fold using your longest stitch length, catching the yarn in the process. (It is helpful to machine baste yarn in place first.)

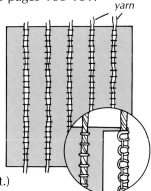

Rolled Edge

A rolled edge is created by changing the width of the stitch finger and adjusting tensions. Consult your serger manual for directions for your model. The resulting stitch makes the fabric roll around a narrower stitch finger.

Three-Thread, Rolled-Edge Tension Adjustments

Tighten the lower looper tension nearly all the way so the lower looper thread forms a straight line on the underside of the fabric. As a result, the upper looper thread will encase the fabric "roll" created over the stitch finger. If the upper looper thread doesn't wrap around the edge, try **loosening** the tension. If it isn't forcing the edge to "roll," try **tightening** the tension.

> **PRO TIP:** If you can't get the lower looper thread tight enough, try texturized nylon in the lower looper. You can also try wrapping the tension dial twice, but do it at your own risk as it is **not** recommended in the manual.

Rolled-edge Stitch Length

A shorter stitch length is usually used for a rolled edge. However, it is best to start at a 2.0mm stitch length and shorten gradually until you achieve the look you like. With a heavy thread like Decor 6, use a stitch length of 2-2.5mm for best results. Sometimes too short a stitch length causes the rolled edge to fall off the fabric, especially along the crosswise grain and on sheer fabrics. When using regular thread for rolled edges on sheers, use a stitch length of 2.5-3.5mm for a soft edge. Hold fabric taut while serging so it doesn't pucker.

Ways to Use Rolled-Edge Finishing

The possibilities for using the rolled edge are limitless! In addition to finishing ruffles, napkin and tablecloth hems, we've used it in the following ways:

Rolled-edge Pin Tucks

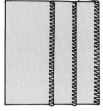

These are created by doing a rolled-edge stitch over a fold. They are most often used in "heirloom serger sewing." See pages 14, 18 and 69-73 for ideas and how-tos.

Serger Piping

Serge over filler cords on a strip of bias tricot "Seams Great" to create custom piping.

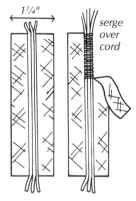

1. Set the machine for a very closely spaced rolled edge (satin stitch), then serge 2"-3" over cords.

2. Place a 1¼"-wide tricot strip under foot and continue serging, leaving a 5/8" width of tricot for easy insertion in a seam.

Rolled-edge Chain

Use rolled-edge chain to create decorator "tassels" (pages 113 and 123), as a "cord" to wrap and tie pillow corners (page 139), and as trim (page 135).

1. Place decorative thread (or threads) in upper looper. This will be the most visible thread in the chain. **Experiment** with thread colors, thicknesses, and combinations.

2. The needle thread is least visible in rolled-edge chain, so use regular serger thread to match decorative thread. Use matching thread, texturized nylon or monofilament nylon thread in lower looper.

3. Adjust tension for rolled edge with chosen threads. For heavier threads, start with a longer stitch (at least 3mm) and shorten gradually until satisfied with stitch appearance. You may have to tighten upper looper tension with slippery threads for a pretty, tightly formed chain stitch.

4. Pull all threads under and at a 45° angle to **left** of presser foot. Hold onto threads to prevent jamming. Stitch, holding chain as it forms to keep stitches smooth and even.

5. For "gutsier" chain, serge over one or more strands of a heavy filler thread such as pearl cotton or yarn.

This section provides the background, basic descriptions and how-to's you need to create your versions of the projects featured in this book. In the introduction on pages 6 and 7, we briefly discussed the planning process in designing a room or an individual home decorating project. We realize that the subject could be a whole book! Here are some of the key elements to consider in your planning.

Home Decorating Fabrics

There is a wide array of wonderful fabrics for home decorating available today. In the past few years, fabrics once obtainable only through professionals, have become readily available at your favorite fabric stores. In addition, more fabric companies are creating coordinating lines that make your room designing a delight. With fabric widths of 54", 60" and the new 90" and even 120", piecing becomes less necessary, cutting down on cost and sewing time.

You'll find a wide variety of fibers and weaves and colors and prints in home decorating fabrics. Keep the following in mind as you make your selections:

- Note care requirements of the fabric you are purchasing. Do you want your project to be washable, or is "dry clean only" okay? Napkins and some other table toppings should be washable and absorbent (to be practical). We would never insist that you ALWAYS be practical!

- Is the fabric sturdy enough for the intended use? Is it soft enough to drape if you want it to drape or crisp enough to hold the desired shape?

- Has it been treated with a stain-repellant finish? (If not, sprays that you can apply are available.)

- If you want a bright or dark color, will it be positioned where direct sunlight will hit it? Some dark colors fade **very** quickly. (Calicos come in a wonderful range of colors and prints, but most just don't like sun.) Red and black are especially susceptible.

- Another color note: Colors can change dramatically when viewed under different lighting. And different fibers and textures reflect light differently. That means two different fabrics that seem to match under the store's fluorescent lighting may not match in daylight or in the warm, nighttime lighting of your home.

- If you are covering existing furniture or pillows, will the fabric require lining to prevent show-through? For durability, long wear, and saving energy, we recommend lining most window coverings.

- Does the fabric have a pattern repeat? If so, measure it! If your project requires piecing (page 150), purchase additional yardage for matching fabric nap, patterns, plaids and one-way stripes.

- How long will the fabric continue to be available? If you are redoing an entire room, you may not want to invest in all the fabric at once, but to guarantee color matching, it's best to buy from the same dye lot. If you find discontinued fabric on sale and you absolutely love it, go for it! Just be aware of the risks. Linda purchased enough fabric for her bedroom window coverings, then decided later to make a quilt. After much searching and then through pure LUCK she found just enough yardage in a remnant at another store months later.

- For serger projects, will the serger handle the weight or thickness of the fabric you are considering? We discovered that some combinations of fabric and decorative thread just didn't work, even though we thought the end result would be wonderful. In these cases, **be flexible**. Some of our best ideas evolved from difficulties!

- When making projects in which the vertical line is important (such as window coverings), be **sure** your fabric is on grain. An off-grain lining fabric drove us **crazy** when making inside-mounted Roman shades! The sides of the shade just wouldn't hang parallel to the sides of the window. Don't buy fabrics that are printed off grain or those that have been pulled off grain during finishing or wrapping on the bolt. Examine carefully and ask the sales clerk for help in determining if the fabric is grain perfect.

How Much Fabric?

Now's the time to dust off those math skills and pull out your pocket calculator. It really isn't difficult!

As you read through the room projects, you will see measuring diagrams for the projects. After selecting a project and before heading to the fabric store, take the measurements and figure the yardage requirements for different fabric widths. Here's how:

1. Make your own "layouts" just like those in pattern instructions. On graph paper, draw 2-yard rectangles to scale to represent widths of 45", 54" and 60" (or 90" or 120" if you are tackling a large project and know that the wider fabrics are available in prints or colors that you like). Make a number of copies of these "master" forms.

2. For each project, sketch out the pieces you'll need—fronts, backs, sides—onto your master. The finished sketch will quickly tell you how many yards you'll need. If piecing is necessary, figure out first to decide how many "lengths" of fabric will be required. The following are some project examples:

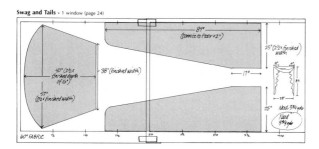

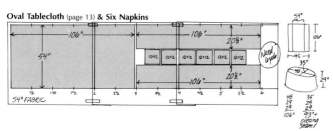

> **NOTE:** Estimated Yardage charts can be obtained from various sources. We have found the ones in the *Instant Interiors* booklets to be very helpful. See page 156.

Remember to take nap, pattern matching (see column at right) and batting or cushion filler loft (page 155) into account when figuring yardage.

Piecing

The primary rule for positioning piecing seams is to make them as inconspicuous as possible. Usually that means on the side, rather than down dead center:

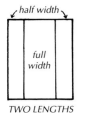
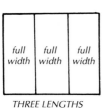
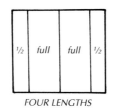

TWO LENGTHS   THREE LENGTHS   FOUR LENGTHS

Whenever possible, piece along selvage edges for the sturdiest results.

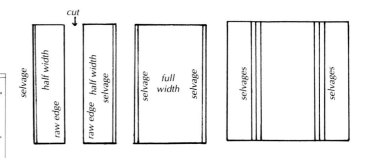

If serging, we recommend a 5-thread machine for seaming. For a really sturdy 3/4- or 3-thread seam, reinforce the serged seam with a row of straight stitching at the seamline.

> **NOTE:** When piecing, remember to add ½" seam allowances to each piece for piecing seams.

Pattern Matching

Printed fabrics have a **design repeat**. On small prints it may be undiscernible. On larger prints it can be as large as 20"-30". **Measure the repeat** on your fabric and add to the required yardage of each length to be pieced.

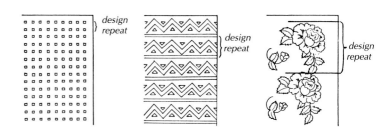

Also check the design repeat across the width of the fabric. Most have an **automatic pattern match.** On some the **usable width** is narrower. On a project like the Quik Trak walls in Pati's bedroom (page 22), a usable width narrower than your fabric would **totally** change the yardage requirements and track positions.

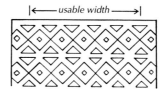
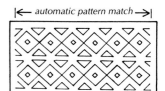

A Home Decorating Glossary

Most of the projects photographed in this book are, no doubt, familiar by sight. But just **what** are they called?

Window Coverings

Roller shades—window coverings made of stiffened fabric fastened to spring-wound rollers, mounted inside window frames. See pages 42, 48, and 58.

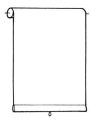

Roman shades - tailored-looking window coverings that fit the shape of the window and pull up into accordion folds with a system of rings and cords. They are usually lined and can be insulated with thermal batting. See pages 33, 55, 66, and 129.

Balloon shades—coverings constructed very much like Roman shades, but because the fabric is also gathered across the top, the look is lush. Variations include **Austrian shades,** (with fixed gathers) and **cloud shades and valances.** See pages 19, 24 and 80.

Cornices—over-the-window treatments constructed of wood or other rigid materials. Some are painted. Ours are fabric-covered. See pages 31, 54, 75 and 80.

Valances—over-the-window fabric treatments. See pages 44, 48, 58, 109 and 120.

Swags and Tails—draped fabric panels that frame a window opening.

Swags drape across the top and can continue partially down the sides. Tails are on the side only. Also referred to as window draping, side drapes and side panels. See pages 10, 24, 66, 86, and 132.

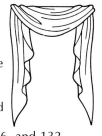

Curtains—the simplest window coverings; each is a rectangle of fabric with a casing at the top for a curtain rod. **Cafe curtains** are mounted halfway down the window (page 103). Sheers are curtains made from sheer fabric (page 10).

Window panels—simple rectangles of fabric. They can be side panels, or actual window coverings. Variations include **window blankets,** which are insulated (page 76), and **tab curtains** (page 91). The **window shades** on page 97 are stiffened like roller shade fabric, but do not roll up and down.

Holdbacks—usually hardware designed to hold a window curtain to the side. They can be as simple as a cup hook or push pin, or as elaborate as designer hardware like the rosettes and tulips from Claesson on page 132. **Tiebacks** are a strips of fabric or cord that pull the curtain to the holdback. They can be found throughout this book in many forms.

Bed Coverings

Comforter—a simple, lined bed covering, frequently filled with batting and quilted. It may drop to the floor or just to the bottom edge of the mattress. See pages 25 and 52.

Quilt—pieced, appliqued or otherwise decorated, quilted comforter. See pages 36, 70, 77 and 128.

Duvet—French for a comforter made of muslin or other utilitarian fabric over batting. Designed to be used inside a **duvet cover.** See pages 40 and 58.

duvet cover

Coverlet (or bedspread, throw)—a bed covering, lined or unlined, and without batting. See page 119.

Afghan—a knit coverlet, often lap-size. Our machine-knit version is on page 37.

Dust ruffle—a bed skirt, usually gathered or pleated, that drops from the top of the boxspring (or equivalent) to the floor along the sides and foot of the bed. See pages 15, 27, 36, and 40, 71 and 119.

Pillow sham—a decorative pillow covering with a back opening. See pages 27, 34, 40 and 53.

Crib bumper—quilted, padded side panels inside a crib. See page 70.

Canopy—fabric draped above and down the corners of a bed. (See pages 14 and 41.)

Furniture

Slipcover—any removable covering for a piece of furniture. Some may be almost as fitted and as tailored as upholstery. We have hired professionals to do this (pages 14, 24, 80 and 129). Others are unconstructed throws (pages 75 and 87).

Box cushions—cushions with "boxing" or side panels, filled with firm foam forms. See pages 66, 111, 130, 134, 138 and 141.

boxing strip

Knife-edge cushions—cushions without separate side panels, filled with foam forms or batting. See pages 15, 36, 96 and 122.

Throw pillows—small cushions scattered in rooms throughout the book, on beds, chairs, and sofa; the variations, shapes and sizes are endless. See index.

Bolster—cylindrical pillow used at the sides or back of beds and sofas. See page 83. Smaller versions are called neck rolls

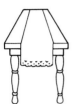

Runner—length of fabric used on upholstered furniture, dressers and tables. Ends hang over one or two sides only.

Sink skirt (pages 44 and 47), **chair skirt** (page 95), **table skirt** (pages 81, 94), and **tree skirt** (page 113).

Tablecloth—any table covering that drapes over the sides (usually round, oval, rectangular, or square). Variations include to-the-floor **table drapes**, **top cloths** or **table toppers**, and **undercloths** (table drapes used underneath table toppers). You'll find them in almost every room!

Placemats—mats to place under individual table settings; can be quilted (page 107 & 110), single- or double-layer (page 115), waterproof (page 101), or fringed (page 107). **Napkins** coordinate with all the table coverings. Dinner napkins are usually 18" square, luncheon napkins, 15", and cocktail napkins, 12."

Floorcloth—a large rectangle of fabric painted with several coats of clear acrylic and used as a rug (page 97).

Accessories and Embellishments

Cozies and scarves—fabric layers that insulate and protect casseroles, breads, mugs (page 104).

Potholder—(page 111).
Jar Covers—(page 111).
Coaster—(page 77).
Desk Accessories—(page 129).
Potpourri Bag—(page 18).
Jewelry Keeper—(page 18).
Covered Box—(pages 19 and 125).

Cord—serged (page 148 and throughout the book), sewn (pages 84-87) and purchased (pages 38, 74, 83).

Tassel—an ornamental tuft of yarns or cords, wrapped and tied together; serged (pages 113 and 123) and purchased (page 72 and 83).

Piping—a narrow tube of fabric trim, made of fabric over cord or by serging a rolled edge over cord (page 148) onto sheer nylon strip (Seams Great). **Welting** is a fatter version and can be either smooth or shirred (page 25). You'll find both used frequently throughout the book.

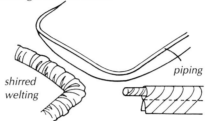

shirred welting   *piping*

Pin tuck—a very narrow, stitched fold in fabric; a detail often found in French hand sewing. You can also do it on a serger (page 70).

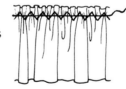

Rosette—soft fabric rose used for tiebacks on sheers and as a decorative detail. See page 12.

Techniques

Gathering—drawing fabric up into a series of close folds. Zigzag over a strong cord.

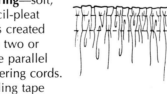

Shirring—soft, pencil-pleat folds created with two or more parallel gathering cords. Gosling tape available in 2- and 3-cord versions.

Smocking—alternating gathered folds created when two or more gathering cords gather opposite segments of fabric.

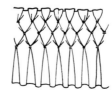

Pleats—flat, folds in fabric that take various forms:

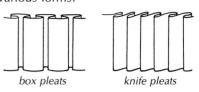

box pleats   *knife pleats*

Fagotting—an open-work decoration in which the thread is drawn across an open seam. We used the serger (pages 12 and 147).

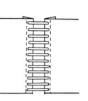

Flanges and Ruffles—decorative tailored and gathered fabric borders used on many home projects.

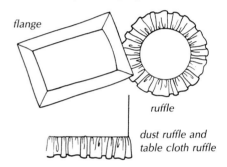

flange   *ruffle*

dust ruffle and table cloth ruffle

Applique—fabric designs and shapes applied to another surface with adhesive products and/or stitching. See pages 16, 44 and 49.

Starching—a fabric application technique developed by Judy Lindahl. Liquid starch is applied to walls or other surface (eg., frames, furniture) and then fabric is pressed into place. Removable. See walls and mirror frame on page 43, decals on boy's room walls, page 57, wall hanging on page 84, and the fabric border on 118. How-to's are on page 46.

Upholstered walls—walls padded and covered with fabric for a luxurious, sound-absorbing effect. Quik Trak (next page, plus 28-29) is easiest installation method.

Channel quilting—parallel rows of machine stitching forming "channels" that can be softly stuffed for quilts, or firmly stuffed for cushions, page 96.

Slipstitch—a hand-sewing stitch to invisibly close seams. Used in pillows and other items that are partially machine seamed, then turned and filled with batting or pillow forms.

Hand catchstitch—a hand-stitch, used for hemming and to piece batting (page 155).

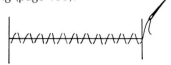

Fabric painting—a versatile embellishment process for creating your own "printed" fabric, and for creating fabrics and motifs that coordinate with purchased prints. Textile designer Suzanne DeVall has developed a line of beautiful, permanent paints that won't stiffen the fabric. See pages 38-42, 83, and 84-87.

Sponge painting—a hand-painting technique using a sponge to create a textured appearance. Used for renovating an old lamp and the fireplace facade in the Ultrasuede Library, pages 126-129 and to refresh the walls in Eleanor's bath, page 14.

The New Notions

As we worked on the rooms in this book we found many wonderful notions that make home decorating projects easier than ever. We wholeheartedly recommend them to you.

Gosling Tapes

These are WONDERFUL! Gathering, shirring, smocking, pleating—all can be done with the pull of a cord (or cords). Gosling's 100% polyester tapes are sewn to flat fabric panels. A tug on the cords pulls the fabric up into the desired form.

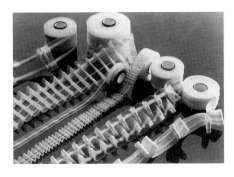

Shirring Tape—a continuous series of even pencil pleats for curtains, tiebacks draperies and valances.

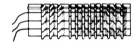

2-Cord Shirring Tape—a narrow shirring tape for gathering fabrics and trims. Also for Austrian shades.

Smocking Tape—a distinctive smocked design for curtains, tieback draperies and valances.

Pleating Tape—a pleated heading for draw draperies and curtains. Install on traverse rods or cafe rods with rings

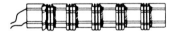

Folding Tape—a narrow, 2-pleat tape for draw draperies. Also makes quick 3" box pleats.

Loop Shade Tape—a transparent shade tape for making Roman, cloud and balloon shades.

NOTE: Subsitute small plastic drapery rings if Loop Shade Tape is unavailable (page 56). Also used on drapery tiebacks, pg 125.

Gosling Cord—fine polyester cord for stringing Roman, cloud, balloon and Austrian shades.

Gosling Hooks—small plastic hooks with prongs that slide into hook loops. Use to hang pleated headings.

General Directions

1. Cut out and prepare fabric as instructed in each project.

2. Pin Gosling tape on wrong side of fabric, making sure the loop side of tape is outside (facing you) and towards the top. Lift cords out of way and turn under raw edges at ends of tape.

3. Stitch tape to fabric along top and bottom edges, being careful not to catch the cords. Knot securely at both sides.

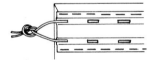

4. Place work on a flat surface; hold cords on one side and use the palm of your hand to gently push fabric to other side as far as it will go without packing. Ease out gathers for needed width. Tie off excess cords and save. (Attach to back of finished piece with pin.) Space gathers evenly across fabric. Complete following project directions.

Adhesives and Fasteners

Sobo glue—white fabric glue that dries clear and remains flexible when dry.

Hot glue gun—a VERY handy tool for many craft projects. We've used it to glue Velcro to sinks (page 44), mirror backs to mirrors (page 18), and foam to bed frames (page 51).

Velcro hook & loop tapes—a fastening system that creates a strong bond and also leaves the item easily removable for laundering. It is available to sew on or with self-adhesive backing. We've used it to attach sink skirts (pages 44 and 47) and dust ruffles (pages 27).

Electric stapler—requires less "elbow grease" than a regular staple gun. Use it to semi-permanently or permanently attach fabric to hard surfaces such as walls. Also invaluable when installing Quik Trak (pages 28-29).

Fusible interfacings—applied with an iron to stiffen and/or reinforce fabric for use as window shades (pages 59 & 97) and floorcloths (page 97). Use Fuse-a-Shade, Create-a-Shade, or, for room darkening, Wonder-Shade. (See Resource List, page 155).

Fusible transfer web—a thin web of heat-sensitive fibers on a sheet of release paper which makes it possible to apply the heat-sensitive material to fabric to create appliques. After removing the paper backing, heat and steam are used to adhere the fabric layers together. Makes appliques a snap. See pages 44, 49, 59 and 66. We also used it to cover accessory boxes (page 19), cardboard building blocks (page 64) and file boxes in the Guestroom/Office (page 125). **Fusible web** is made of similar heat-sensitive fibers, but without the backing so application method varies.

Liquid starch—used for starching fabric to walls and other surfaces. See previous page. Purchase bottled starch at grocery store.

Fray Check— liquid seam sealant; you can't do without it! Use to seal serger tails and thread knots.

Quik Trak™

This wall upholstery system is a unique product introduced to home sewers by Brad Hartley and Ann Thomassen. This adhesive-backed plastic track creates "stretcher frames" on walls and other surfaces. You easily "snap" fabric panels into place.

For how-tos see pages 28 & 29 in the chapter on Pati's bedroom. For more Quik Trak projects, see pages 38-42, the folding screen on pages 98-99, and the library walls upholstered in Ultrasuede Facile on pages 126-129.

Battings and Fillers

These foams and fibers have a myriad of uses in home decorating, from pillows and quilts to walls, potholders, furniture and window coverings. We used products from Hobbs in the rooms —quilt batting, batting by the yard for walls, pillow forms of all shapes and sizes. Substitute polyester fleece, such as Thermolam, for puffier batting products when a thin, firm padding is desired.

If you want to create insulated window coverings, use Warm Window and Warm Winter battings (pages 55, 66, 76 and 91.)

Batting is available in pre-cut quilt sizes and by the yard and comes in different "lofts" or thicknesses. Choose the loft that works best for your project; its OK to use several layers. Take desired loft into account when measuring and cutting the project.

width of fabric to include "take-up" allowance - can be as much as 13" on king size comforter.

finished width

When piecing batting, do not overlap edges. Butt edges and hand catchstitch to hold in place.

Ann Thomassen of Quik Trak snaps fabric into place.

Quik Trak strips, ends cut at a 45° angle, form a frame on the wall.

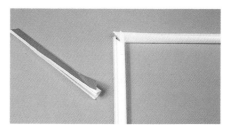

Peel off paper backing to expose adhesive tape. Press against wall surface to adhere; staple to secure.

Staple batting in place.

Snap fabric into place, beginning along top edge.

Resources/Bibliography

The Fabrics

Ask for these fabrics used in the book at your favorite fabric store. If you can not find them and wish to contact the manufacturer directly, please call us at (503) 294-0696 for the necessary information.

Concord Fabrics
English Garden Polished Apple (pages 30, 47, 78)
Christmas Elegance (114)

Creative Home Textiles
Torrence Place Collection (108)
Scheherazade (126)

Fabric Traditions
Cabana (93), Scarborough (136), Arabesque (74), Coco's Kids (57)

Lace Country
Morning Glories (98), French Rose (8), Fine Rose (98), Tulip and Cats (102)

Spartex Fabrics
Doublecloth™ (30, 84)
Doubleglaze™ (38)

Springs Industries, Inc.
90" Grand Elegance Collection & Petite Elegance coordinates (22)
Wamsutta Christmas Gathering(66)

Ultrasuede Brand Fabrics
Ultrasuede and Facile (83, 84, 100,126)

V.I.P. a division of
Cranston Print Works Company
When I Grow Up (62)
Stratford Hall (117)

Waverly Fabrics
Rosie Collection (43)
Spring Garden (8)

Daisy Kingdom (50)
134 NW 8th Ave.
Portland, OR 97209
503/222-9033
This retail store based in Portland has a mail order catalog.

The Products

These are the products we used in the book. If your local store does not carry them, these companies can refer you to the closest retailer. Or give your favorite retailer the information and they can order it for you!

The Claesson Company, Inc.
P.O. Box 130
Cape Neddick, ME 03902
207/363-5059 or 800/344-9128
Claesson's Magic swag holder (132) and other window hardware

E.E. Schenck Co.
P.O. Box 5200
Portland, OR 97208
800/433-0722
Lampshade frames

Gosling Tapes®
1814 Marian Ave.
Thousand Oaks, CA 91360
805/493-1387
Also: EZ International
95 Mayhill Street
Saddlebrook, NJ 07662
201/712-1234
Smocking, Pleating, Shirring, Folding & Loop Shade tapes and non-stretchy cord (see index)

Hobbs Bonded Fibers
P.O. Box 151
Groesbeck, TX 76642
800/433-3357
High quality white and grey quilt batting of all weights and sizes; batting by the yard for upholstering walls; and pillow forms of all sizes and shapes (see index)

Hollywood Trims
305 Montford Avenue, Suite 3
Mill Valley, CA 94941
415/381-4833
Trims, tassels, braids, cords and fringe (83, 74). Inquire about their printed pamphlets and booklets on trim projects and tips.

Quik Trak
84 Reservoir Park Dr.
Rockland, MA 02370
800/872-8725
Quik Trak (22, 28-29, 38, 126)
Folding Screen (98)
*For their 32 page booklet on **Easy Home Decorating With Quik Trak**, send $4.50.*

Suzanne DeVall Paints
2726 NE 14th
Portland, OR 97212
503/284-1160
Su-Tek™ fabric paints, foam brushes and instructional video (38, 83, 84, 88). Write for information about workshops.

Velcro USA, Inc.
P.O. Box 5218
406 Brown Ave.
Manchester, NH 03108
603/669-4892
Sew-in and Sticky-Back® Velcro®; 1½" wide Velcro® (see index)

Warm Products, Inc.
16120 Woodinville-Redmond Rd. #5
Woodinville, WA 98072
800/234-WARM
Patented insulating fabrics: Warm Winter® 1000,3000 and 5000, and complete patented Warm Window® system (see index)

Foamcore foam-centered board is available at art supply stores.

These products were mentioned generically in the book:

Shade Backings:
Fuse-A-Shade™ by HTC
Create A Shade by Dritz
Wonder-Shade™ by Pellon®
Presto® by Harpers

Transfer Webs:
Magic Fuse by Dritz
Trans-Web™ by H.T.C.
Wonder-Under™ and Heavy Duty Wonder-Under™ by Pellon
Like Magic® by Harpers
Heat'n Bond by Therm'o Web

Patterns

Becky's Homespun Creations
20832 SE Morrison
Gresham, OR 97030
503/667-5577
rag doll pattern

Klaus B. Rau Company
P.O. Box 1236
Coeur d'Alene, ID 83814
My Own Teepee

The McCall Pattern Company
See their catalog in your favorite
fabric store.

**Speedy The Cat,
A Good Friends Company**
P.O. Box 3439
Salem, OR 97302
503/362-5969
circus tent

Accessories

Mamma Ro'
P.O. Box 12046
Portland, OR 97212
503/274-0686
Imported handmade Italian dinner-
ware and glassware (108, 114, 136).

Threads

A&E Thread Mills
P.O. Box 507
Mount Holly, NC 28120
704/827-4311
Serger thread

Coats and Clark
P.O. Box 24998
Greenville, S.C. 29616
803/234-0331
Sewing and serger thread
#5 Pearl Cotton

DMC
107 Trumbull St.
Elizabeth, NY 07206
201/351-4550
#8 Pearl Cotton

Gutermann of America
8227 Arrowridge Blvd.
Charlotte, NC 28273
800/528-5187
High quality sewing thread and silk
thread

Rhode Island Textile Co.
P.O. Box 999
Pawtucket, RI 02862
401/722-3700
Ribbon Floss

Specialty serger threads such as
Decor 6, Woolly nylon, and
Candlelight is available through
Palmer/Pletsch Associates

Mail Order Catalogs

Mail order catalogues are another
source of items unavailable locally.

Clotilde, Inc.
1909 SW First Ave.
Fort Lauderdale, FL 33315-2100
305/761-8655

Nancy's Notions
P.O. Box 683
Beaver Dam, WI 53916
414/887-0391

The Perfect Notion
566 Hoyt Street
Darien, CT 06820
203/968-1257

Books and Booklets

Instant Interiors Publishing
P.O. Box 1793
Eugene, OR 97440
*Bed Covers, Easiest Furniture
Covers, Fabric Space Makers,
Lampshades, Pillows, Quickest
Curtains, Table Toppings*

Slipcovers and Bedspreads
A Sunset book
Lane Publishing
Menlo Park, CA

For Palmer/Pletsch books and Judy
Lindahl's books, see pages 159 and
160.

Custom Sewing

PACC (The Professional Association
of Custom Clothiers) is a newly
formed organization made up of
sewing professionals around the
country. To find a home decorating
or slipcover specialist, or to be
included yourself in the nation-wide
listing, write PACC, 1375 Broadway,
NY, NY 10018.

Metric Conversions
(slightly rounded)

1/8" = 3 mm	1/8 yd = .12 m
1/4" = 6 mm	1/4 yd = .23 m
3/8" = 10 mm or 1 cm	3/8 yd = .35 m
1/2" = 13 mm or 1.3 cm	1/2 yd = .46 m
5/8" = 15 mm or 1.5 cm	5/8 yd = .58 m
3/4" = 20 mm or 2 cm	3/4 yd = .69 m
7/8" = 22 mm or 2.2 cm	7/8 yd = .81 m
1" = 25 mm or 2.5 cm	1 yd = .92 m

Index

ADDITIONAL PRODUCTS FROM PALMER/PLETSCH

Palmer/Pletsch publishes easy to use, information-filled sewing how-to books. Look for our books and videos in local fabric stores or order through Palmer/Pletsch.

BOOKS

☐ **The Serger Idea Book**—A Collection of Inspiring Ideas from Palmer/Pletsch, *8½"×11", 160 pgs., $18.95* Color photos and how-to's on inspiring and fashionable ideas from the Extraordinary to the Practical.

☐ **Creative Serging for the Home**—And Other Quick Decorating Ideas, *by Lynette Ranney Black and Linda Wisner, 8½"×11", 160 pgs., $18.95* Color photos and how-to's to help you transform your home into the place you want it to be.

☐ **Sewing With Sergers**—The Complete Handbook for Overlock Sewing, *by Pati Palmer & Gail Brown, 128 pgs., $6.95* Learn easy threading tips, stitch types, rolled edging and flatlocking on your serger.

☐ **Creative Serging**—The Complete Handbook for Decorative Overlock Sewing, *by Pati Palmer, Gail Brown & Sue Green, 128 pgs., $6.95* In-depth information and creative uses of your serger.

☐ **Creative Serging Illustrated,** *by Pati Palmer, Gail Brown & Sue Green, 160 pgs., $14.95* Same content as Creative Serging PLUS color photography.

☐ **Sew to Success!**—How to Make Money in a Home-Based Sewing Business, *by Kathleen Spike, 128 pgs., $10.95* Learn how to establish your market, set policies and procedures, price your talents and more!

☐ **Mother Pletsch's Painless Sewing,** *Revised Edition, by Pati Palmer & Susan Pletsch, 128 pgs., $6.95* The most uncomplicated sewing book of the century! Filled with sewing tips on how to sew FAST!

☐ **Sensational Silk**—A Handbook for Sewing Silk and Silk-like Fabrics, *by Gail Brown, 128 pgs., $6.95* Complete guide for sewing with silkies from selection to perfection in sewing.

☐ **Pants For Any Body,** *Revised Edition, by Pati Palmer & Susan Pletsch, 128 pgs., $6.95* Learn to fit pants with clear step-by-step problem and solution illustrations.

☐ **Sewing Ultrasuede® Brand Fabrics**—Ultrasuede®, Facile®, Caress™, Ultraleather™, *by Marta Alto, Pati Palmer and Barbara Weiland, 8½"×11", 128 pages, $16.95.* Inspiring color fashion photo section, plus the newest techniques to help you master these luxurious fabrics.

☐ **Easy, Easier, Easiest Tailoring,** *Revised Edition, by Pati Palmer and Susan Pletsch, 128 pgs., $6.95* Learn 4 different tailoring methods, easy fit tips, and timesaving machine lining.

☐ **Clothes Sense**—Straight Talk About Wardrobe Planning, *by Barbara Weiland & Leslie Wood, 128 pgs., $6.95* Learn to define your personal style and when to sew or buy.

☐ **Sew a Beautiful Wedding,** *by Gail Brown & Karen Dillon, 128 pgs., $6.95* Bridal how-to's on choosing the most flattering style to sewing with specialty fabrics.

☐ **Decorating with Fabric: An Idea Book,** *by Judy Lindahl, 128 pgs., $6.95* Learn to cover walls, create canopies, valances, pillows, lamp shades, and more!

☐ **The Shade Book,** *by Judy Lindahl, 128 pgs., $6.95* Learn six major shade types and variations of them, trimmings, hardware, hemming, care, and upkeep.

☐ **Energy Saving Decorating,** *by Judy Lindahl, 128 pgs., $6.95* Thoroughly researched techniques for energy efficient windows and walls.

☐ **Original Roo** (The Purple Kangaroo), *by Bob Benz, 48 pgs., $4.95* A whimsical children's story about a kangaroo's adventures and how she saves the day with sewing.

Also available spiralbound—$3.00 additional for large books, $2.00 for small.

VIDEOS

According to Robbie Fanning, author and critic, "The most professional of all the (video) tapes we've seen is Pati Palmer's Sewing Today the Time Saving Way. This tape should serve as the standard of excellence in the field." Following that standard, we have produced 6 more videos since Time Saving! *Videos are $29.95 each.*

☐ **Sewing Today the Time Saving Way,** 45 minutes featuring Lynn Raasch & Karen Dillon sharing tips and techniques to make sewing fun, fast and trouble free.

☐ **Sewing to Success,** 45 minutes featuring Kathleen Spike who presents a wealth of information on how to achieve financial freedom working in your home as a professional dressmaker.

☐ **Sewing With Sergers — Basics,** 1 hour featuring Marta Alto & Pati Palmer on tensions, stitch types and their uses, serging circles, turning corners, gathering and much more.

☐ **Sewing With Sergers—Advanced,** 1 hour featuring Marta Alto & Pati Palmer on in depth how-to's for rolled edging & flatlocking as well as garment details.

☐ **Creative Serging,** 1 hour featuring Marta Alto & Pati Palmer on how to use decorative threads, yarns and ribbons on your serger. PLUS: fashion shots!

☐ **Creative Serging II,** 1 hour featuring Marta Alto & Pati Palmer showing more creative ideas, including in-depth creative rolled edge.

☐ **Sewing Ultrasuede Brand Fabrics—Ultrasuede, Facile, Caress, Ultraleather,** 1 hour featuring Marta Alto and Pati Palmer with clear, step-by-step sewing demonstrations and fashion show.

TRENDS BULLETINS

Trends Bulletins are comprehensive 8-12 page two-color publications designed to keep you up-to-date by bringing you the best and the newest information on all your favorite sewing topics.

☐ **The Newest in Sewing Room Design,** *by Lynette Ranney Black.* This is the handbook for designing a sewing room covering, proper sewing and pressing heights, layout styles, lighting and more! *$3.50*

☐ **The Newest in Ultrasuede Brand Fabrics,** *by Marta Alto & Ann Price,* gives pattern selection guidance, layout, cutting, and sewing of the new Facile, Caress and Ultraleather. *$3.50*

☐ **Trends in Decorative Threads for the Serger,** *by Ann Price,* gives the most up-to-the minute information on decorative threads including how and where to use them. *$3.50*

☐ **Knitting Machines—An Introduction,** *by Terri Burns,* presents the basics of machine knitting, including stitch patterns, explanation of single and double bed machines, and a step-by-step guide to making your purchasing decision. *$3.95*

☐ **Interfacings,** *by Ann Price,* sorts out all the recent changes, presenting a clear picture of the interfacings available today and how best to make use of them. *$3.95*

Palmer/Pletsch also offers seminars and workshops around the U.S.A. and Canada. Extensive 4-day workshops for the avid sewer are held in Portland, Oregon.

We also carry hard to find and unique notions including Decor 6 Rayon thread and Henckels scissors. Thread color cards are available for $2.00. Check your local fabric store or contact Palmer/Pletsch Associates, P.O. Box 12046, Portland, OR 97212-0046. (503) 274-0687.